Charles Aurand

Rays of light

Lectures on great subjects

Charles Aurand

Rays of light
Lectures on great subjects

ISBN/EAN: 9783337270643

Printed in Europe, USA, Canada, Australia, Japan

Cover: Foto ©Andreas Hilbeck / pixelio.de

More available books at **www.hansebooks.com**

RAYS OF LIGHT;

OR

LECTURES ON GREAT SUBJECTS.

BY

CHARLES MONROE AURAND,

PASTOR OF EVANGELICAL LUTHERAN CHRIST CHURCH,
TRENTON, N. J.

PUBLISHED FOR THE AUTHOR.

LUTHERAN PUBLICATION SOCIETY,
PHILADELPHIA, PA.

TABLE OF CONTENTS.

(iii)

iv

PREFACE.

THE author believes that the existence of this volume is justified by two facts :

First. The laity of the Christian Church need information touching the subjects herein discussed. Scientists furnish scientific facts, philosophers supply philosophic truths, but the whole world looks to the ministers of Jesus Christ for knowledge concerning the deep things of God and man. The ministerial office is entrusted with two functions, namely, *preaching* and *teaching*. The first makes its appeal mainly to the conscience and will, and is evangelistic, while the latter addresses the intellect, and is designed to edify and nurture the evangelized.

An extended observation forces the writer to the conclusion that the teaching function, in the majority of pulpits, does not measure up to the needs, nor to the desires, of the pew—that many of God's people "perish for lack of knowledge." Christian people have a right to look to their spiritual guides for instruction upon the "inner meaning " of the great themes of Divine Revelation.

Second. So far as the writer's acquaintance with books extends, he does not know of any volume which covers the field occupied by this manual, suited to the wants of the laity. The standard theological tomes are indispensable to the divinity student, but remain unappreciated and unread by the busy layman.

The opinion is cherished, therefore, that the "rays of light " focused in these "lectures on great subjects" will not be entirely unwelcome and unprofitable to those to whom they are dedicated.

The style of direct address is due to the fact that these lectures were originally delivered before the author's congregation substantially as they stand here.

No high claims of any kind are set up for this messenger of light, except that every paragraph has been written in prayer for the Holy Spirit's guidance and counsel: and now may the divinest blessings of the triune God be vouchsafed to all who may read what has been written!

C. M. A.

Trenton, N. J., October, 1890.

LECTURE I.

THE CREATION OF MAN.

GEN. i. 29.

Gen. i. *29.*   So God created Man in His own image.

LECTURE I.

THE study of man is both attractive and important. It is second only to the study of God. In truth, these two subjects are so coupled together that by putting aside one, the other loses all interest and force. It is the purpose of the author to contribute, in successive lectures, somewhat to the end of a correct understanding of him who was created in the image of God. In reading the account of creation as found in the first and second chapters of Genesis, we are impressed with a few things that seem very striking.

First, touching the manner of man's creation. With reference to all the other departments of God's works the simple language is used: "Let there be light, and there was light." "Let there be a firmament in the midst of the waters, and let it divide the waters from the waters." "Let the water under the heaven be gathered together into one place, and let the dry land appear, and it was so." "Let there be lights in the firmament of the heaven to divide the day from the night, and let

2   (9)

them be for signs and for seasons, and for days
and for years." The same terms are employed all
the way through, down to the work of the sixth
day—the creation of man.

Now, at this point, there is an evident departure
from the foregoing. It matters not what our interpretation may be of this departure, the fact itself remains. The language: "Let us make man
in our image, after our likeness, and let them have
dominion over the fish of the sea, and over the
fowls of the air, and over the cattle, and over all
the earth, and over every creeping thing that
creepeth upon the earth," stands out as prominent
as the noonday sun, and is surely very impressive.

Certainly nothing new is put forth in the remark that this peculiar expression seems to intimate a plurality in the distinction of the Godhead
—*Trinity in unity*. This is the sober interpretation by the profoundest minds, and has been advanced as a proof-text by trinitarians from the
very beginning of theological discussion. Such
interpretation manifestly falls in with the analogy
of faith concerning this doctrine.

*Another circumstance in relation to man's cre-
ation is, that he was last to come from the hand
of the Almighty.* All things else were made, and

then last and greatest of all comes man. "He
was the last as well as the finest of the Divine
works. His residence, and all other things necessary for his comfort, were prepared for his reception. Then, when the earth had been fashioned
in all its beauty, and Eden enriched with all her
stores of enjoyment, God made man, the climax
of creating wisdom, power and love."

*Once more, man stands highest in the scale of
creation.* While on one side he is related to the
earth, on the other he is linked to heaven.

The seventh verse of the second chapter of Genesis reads, "And the Lord God formed man out of
the dust of the ground, and breathed into his
nostrils the breath of life, and man became a living soul."

In the mechanism and functions of the body,
scientists tell us there is a close and striking re-
semblance to that of the bodies of animals. Indeed, this fact has of late years been made so
prominent that there are not a few to-day who
make bold to assert that the material part of man
is *all there is of him.* Almost every school boy is
more or less acquainted with the theory of evolution—for it has poisoned the very atmosphere—
which hypothesis develops man from the ape, and

the ape from something before it, and so on back
to the Moneron, which is said to be the lowest
but also the first living thing, from which therefore all animal existence springs, and from which
all species of animals are developed by laws inherent in *nature*. If it be asked, "Whence did
the first germ of life come?" different answers will
be returned, according to the theological position
of the person questioned. If he be a theist, the
answer is, "From God." If he be an .atheist,
the response will be, "Spontaneous Generation,"
or else the question will be evaded altogether.
Again, if we interrogate respecting the laws governing the development of the different species,
some answer: "They are the orderly and fixed
method of God's activity in the natural world;"
while others, classifying and naming them as
"natural selection," "survival of the fittest,"
"struggle for existence," "environment" and
"heredity," declare: "These laws themselves
have been decreed and developed by the exigency
of the universe, and that is all there is to be said
about them."

It is certainly reasonable that we should consider the similarity existing between the make-up
and functions of the body, "made out of the dust

of the ground," and that of the lower creatures. Doing this, however, does not close our eyes to some striking dissimilarities—among many others such, for example, as these : Man is the only creature that walks upright, facing heavenward ; he is the only being on earth with physical organs of speech ; and he also stands alone in mind functions, for rational and responsible mental activity.

In respect to the bodily parts which man and beast have in common with each other, no one needs to be driven to the fixed conclusion that the materialistic theory of evolution is the last word that can be spoken in explanation of them. Why is not the Duke of Argyle right when he says that "it is reasonable to suppose that God created all bodies after the same general type?" It would, I say it reverently, look almost like child's play— and certainly it would seem to indicate creative activity without creative plan or order—to form one body or species according to one plan, and another according to a different plan, and still another further different, and so on endlessly. Our notion of the wisdom of God supports the idea that all bodies were created after the same general type, whether of man or beast, *so far as their functions are identical*, and that only where an additional function or functions are added, as in man, are there to be found additional physical organs and apparatuses, which in some cases may seem to be like a real departure from the common plan.

As it is not within the scope of this address, so it is not my object, to say anything, either in defence or opposition, of the "development theory." That task is in better hands than mine. But as a somewhat earnest and close student of biology for a period of ten years, tracing out all sides and phases of the subject, I come back with the full and satisfying conviction that man was created by the direct and immediate fiat of God. While there may have been, and most likely were, natural developments in some departments of the creation, I, for one, do not claim the glory of belief in evolution, as that term is used in scientific circles. I am also persuaded that the simple faith of our forefathers, on this subject, *is the best faith still for all those whom I am addressing.*

Dropping the matter of man's physical nature, and renewing my remark that he is the most exalted being in the creative scale, it is not without truth to say that he is such, most particularly, on account of his spiritual nature. More of this pres-

ently. Suffice it to say here that man was formed
to bridge the chasm between pure animal and pure
spirit. He is the middle link between animated
creatures of the earth and the celestial host of
heaven — *a material, immaterial, earth-born and
heaven-begotten creature.*

I have now come to a point in the discussion of
the subject in hand, when it is proper to institute
further inquiries touching what I regard as the
real meaning of it. I am not ignorant of the fact
that it is more *interesting* than *easy* to address one's-
self to this task; and in the presence of the war of
tongues that has been waged around this theme, it
is not easy to say the last word, and thus bring
about cessation of arms. However, the Holy
Ghost can bring light out of darkness, and harmony out of discord, and we have the assurance
that if we desire to know the truth, and look to
Him, He will teach us. Under the inspiration of
this promise I proceed.

"So God created man in His own image."

What can be the meaning of the last word in the
above sentence? I am safe in saying—for I speak
from former personal experience—that by far the
major part of the "common people" take this
word as meaning that man, in his external, vis-

ible person, resembles the person or being of God.
That is to say, that God took his own form as the
model after which he fashioned the body of man,
*and thus he is made in God's image and likeness.
Now this is not the primary and fundamental
meaning of this term.* At the same time, I am
compelled to give my firm conviction on this phase
of the meaning of this word, and right here will I
likely evoke the criticism of many learned doctors.

I need hardly say that I have long ago put aside
all merely traditional belief, and that I have tried
to study this subject, or phase of subject, from an
independent, or perhaps I should say, scientific
and philosophic standpoint.

The result of such study leads me to affirm that
for all I or any one else can say to the contrary,
there may be truth in the home-spun notion of
every-day people. I know of no better place than
this to express my personal opinion, not only neg-
atively, but also positively, *that man's outer form
does partake of the similitude of his Creator's form.*
I number myself among those who hold to the
doctrine that our physical frame is an exact counterpart of the soul. That the soul, so to speak, is
the pattern on which the body is framed—part corresponding to part, and the whole *external* and

visible in harmony with the whole *internal* and *invisible*.

To me, the received opinion that we know not what the soul of man is, that we are ignorant of its shape and form—if it is square, or round, or oblong, or circular, or what not—whether it has eyes and ears, nose and mouth, hands and feet—is positively repugnant, because it is absolutely unsatisfactory. Certainly to my mind it is trifling with a most serious subject. Such quibbling is not only vague and cloudy, but entirely unworthy of great thinkers.

Now admitting that we cannot scientifically demonstrate the human shape of the soul (neither does science even establish the *existence* of the soul), this idea does seem to be the legitimate conclusion of Christian philosophy, and surely it is the decision of one of the best of all judges, viz., Common Sense.

This theory has, to say the very least, and the opposite theory has not, something definite and fixed and satisfying to support it, and it will consequently hold an increasingly high and prominent place in the human mind.

It is not without profit to state that it is only in the light of this truth that many of the physical phenomena can be reasonably explained.

I now come back to my original proposition, namely, that perhaps after all there "are more things than we dream of in our philosophy" in the common folk version of man's being created in the image of God. All that I have so far said is by no means proof positive of the truthfulness of such version, still I do declare that construct- ively I come to that conclusion. Putting pheno- mena by the side of phenomena, and placing fact with fact, and comparing principle with principle, of things which we know and admit, and others which we take on the authority of the Bible, as a good and faithful judge we *infer the truth that man, even as to form, is created in the image of God.*

I speak only for myself when I say, *commend me to a Father who is determinate in form and definite in every organ of his infinite being.* Such a Maker comes within my mental grasp—so far as it is pos- sible for the infinite to be comprehended by the finite—and not only so, but in love and admiration will I be able some day to literally fall on His neck, to bless and praise Him for my eternal salva- tion *in His presence,* where there is fulness of joy, and at His *right hand,* where there are pleasures forevermore. I have to say just a word more before I dismiss this part of my thesis, and that is, that the foregoing position is the only one that will keep us from landing in pantheism. It admits the *immanence in nature of God's power and wisdom;* but it commends itself still more by *lifting above nature the determinate, personal Creator.*

Some time ago I remarked that the similarity of man's form with that of God, *is not the primary and fundamental meaning of the word "image" and "likeness."* I here repeat that assertion. The primary, and at the same time the truest and sublimest meaning, lies in the direction of spiritual capacities and powers. In one word, man is created in the "image of God" because he enjoys similar intellectual and emotional and volitional powers and functions.

Physically animal, man possesses also the mental parts of the same, *but spiritually divine,* he possesses also the faculties (not perfections, in the fullest sense of that term) of divinity. So it is written of him in the "volume of the book" that he is just a little lower than the angels. The explanation of this is at hand. Angels are pure spirits, and do not in any way participate in the animal nature— are, accordingly, in so far higher than man; or, which is the same thing put in a different way,

man does participate in the animal economy, and is
therefore, in so far, just a little lower than the
angels.

Angels being created by the same God, received
upon them the stamp of divinity, the same as man.
In this respect there is no difference between
these two classes of beings, they having the same
spiritual capacities, inasmuch as both are modeled
after their Maker's perfections. At the same time
it may be fair to conclude that though man had
continued in his original Edenic purity, he would
not, while in the flesh, and on that very account,
enjoy the *same highly developed powers as angels.*
The "flesh" being coupled with the "spirit"
hedges and limits the latter's enlargement. Following our analogy, I feel to say that as soon as
man escapes the flesh—or, what amounts to the
same thing,—when the flesh itself is glorified,—he
becomes free to go on and on and still on to endless perfecting, never reaching the height of his
infinite Creator, but possibly reaching, and perhaps
in some matters transcending, the status of the
angelic hosts.

I have said that at least one version of the term
"image" is found in the fact of similarity of
spiritual capacities and powers between the creature and the Creator.

I deem it proper to inquire at this juncture, what are these? I answer, using the nomenclature of Kant and others, *Reason*, Rational and Spiritual Susceptibilities, and Will in Liberty. I must chiefly content myself with this bare statement, for I am admonished of the fact that while the field thus opened is supremely tempting to my mental trend, I must forego the great pleasure it would afford me to go in and "taste and see," in order to confine myself to the scope of my "fore-ordained" plan to address you in as concise and simple a way as possible. Still I cannot leave this vital and interesting part of my subject without indicating a few thoughts, in fuller elucidation of what lies in my mind.

In the first place, I confess to inability to trace the plain line of demarkation running between animal mind and the human mind. Perhaps, indeed, there is no "plain line" between the two; nevertheless there is a line. In stamping the animal mind, I think the Creator wrote: "So far and no farther; here must thy proud waves (of thinking, feeling and willing) be stopped." Touching the human mind he wrote: "Roll on *ceaselessly and endlessly.*"

Allow me to classify the mental functions in which the two agree:

1. Animals have Sense. This is the intellectual realm in which there is the operation of the five senses: sight, hearing, smell, taste and touch. Through the respective organs, of which the above are the functions, the animal has sensation and perception. In other words, through these organs there is contact with the outer world, and a knowledge of its phenomena is obtained. These same functions are present in man. Some of these functions may be more highly developed, and certainly some not as highly, as in the brute, and consequently his sensations and perceptions may be keener or less keen, in proportion to the capacity of the senses.

2. The animal and man alike possess the Understanding. By this intellectual power, knowledge is gained of the things underlying phenomena, viz., substance. If it be true, according to the teaching of many profound minds, that by the Sense there can be no knowledge of the things that cause and occasion "appearances," it is also true that by the additional and higher attribute, the Understanding, such further knowledge is secured.

This superadded perfection involves a number of co-ordinate faculties, such as these: Abstrac-

tion, Reflection, Association, Memory, Induction
and Deduction.

That the animal has all these faculties, is
plainly evident when their habits and conduct are
closely studied. It is true that as these faculties
inhere in the brute creation, they are usually
known as instinct. Now instinct is more properly
classed among the *feelings*, at least some so class
it; but while *feeling* may give the impulse for
conduct, the beginning and middle and end of instinct is knowledge—knowledge, too, that is of
the same nature with that which is gained by
the faculties of the Understanding, above enumerated. I do not 'assert that the brute consciously employs these powers, for this I do not
believe, as by its endowment it may go straight
to the result without its processes; but what I do
believe and aver is, that the animal's knowledge
is of a piece with that which is acquired when
those faculties are consciously used, as in man.

In order that I may not offend, I desire to say
that while brute knowledge, in the sphere of the
Understanding, *is certainly greater in some directions, it is also certainly much inferior in many
more directions, to that of man.*

In the matter of memory, induction and deduc-

tion, I affirm positively that the Understanding in
man towers high above that of the brute, being
reinforced, as it is, by another and higher attribute, of which I will presently speak — the
Reason.

The Sense and the Understanding are the only
intellectual powers identical in animal and man.
We now pass on from the Intellect to the Susceptibility in both.

Philosophers declare that the emotive capacity
depends on the intellectual capacity, and as the
intellect goes out into activity, so will also the
emotive nature go out—the latter in response to
and in harmony with the former. This I presume
is true.

It follows, therefore, that there must be an
emotive capacity in both animal and man to cor-
respond and square with their intellectual nature.
For every intellectual department or faculty, as
the Sense and the Understanding in animal, and
the Sense and the Understanding and the Reason
in man, there is an emotive department, or capacity, to agree as a counterpart, so to speak, with
the intellectual nature.

This last sentence, in general, is true, but it
needs some explanation. As we shall see pres-

ently, man is not only an intellectual being, but in and with that intellect is wrapped up a spiritual nature. Now the only point I want to make here with this anticipatory statement is this, that the Sense and the Understanding, which we have found to exist in the brute creation, do not have their exact emotive counterparts in the Susceptibility.

The great American philosopher, Dr. Hickok, names three distinct divisions in the capacity for feeling, viz., Animal, Rational, and Spiritual. Now it seems clear, from what I have already intimated, that the division called the Spiritual Susceptibility fits in with the spiritual element of man, and corresponds with and responds to spiritual-intellectual activities. The next lower division, named the Rational Susceptibility, is the emotive capacity chiefly set over against the activity of the Reason in the intellectual. It, therefore, simply remains to be said that the next lower and remaining division, the Animal Susceptibility, is matched and covered by the two intellectual faculties, the Sense and the Understanding. From this we see that the only susceptibility common to animal and man, at least in its entirety, is the *Animal Susceptibility*.

Now in this division we find the following par-

3

ticular feelings: the instincts, the appetites, natural affection, self-interested feelings, and disinterested feelings. Some writers give more and some less; some class them according to one divisive principle and others according to another. The above is the number and order given by Dr. Hickok, and so far as my personal study of the subject extends, I can see no reason for dissenting from this classification.

In concluding this subject, I have to repeat what I remarked under the head of the understanding. It was this: the brute's *knowledge*, up to a certain point—to the limit of its faculties—is as great, generally speaking, as that of man. This assertion, adapted to this subject, is equally true. The *feelings* of the animal, up to a certain point —to the limits of the Animal Susceptibility—are just as intense as those of man.

If the animal has an Intellect and a Susceptibility, so also has it a Will.

All that needs to be said on this subject can be spoken in a few words.

Brute will is nothing more nor less than an executive act to gratify feelings. Knowledge of an object calls forth feelings, either favorable or unfavorable to that object; and those in turn evoke the agency of the mind to appropriate or else put away the object, according as the feelings are favorable or otherwise. The executive activity of the mind, without any real choice or alternative, is Animal Will. Man, having similar intellectual and emotive capacities, of course also necessarily has a like Will.

To satisfy his constitutional wants and desires, his mind will reach out (through the medium of his body) toward appropriating the object of gratification. Now note this fact. The object that will best satisfy this want and gratify this desire must be selected. Man's whole being, up to this point, is so thoroughly constitutional and carnal that his executive agency can go out only in one direction, and that is, "fulfilling the desires of the flesh, with the lusts thereof."

I have now, in as small a compass as possible, endeavored to exhibit the likeness of animal and man. This constitutes only the background of what follows. What has been said of man is by no means the last word. He is only now, like the morning sun, rising above the horizon. The Spirit breaking through the flesh, his glory now begins to shine. "A little lower than the angels." "So God created man in his own image."

It must be patent to you all that so far we have
not yet discovered the "likeness of God" in man.
I remark, however, that while our opinion of him
may not be very exalted so far, it is this very part
of his being that fits him for existence and activity
on the earth. Pure spirits cannot get on among
earthly and material things. Thanks be to God,
that His image is superinduced upon man's carnal
nature.

Going back, and taking up the Intellect, we at
once recognize the Divine image in what most
psychologists call the Reason. Now, what is the
province and prerogative of the reason? Simply
this: It peers beneath, above and beyond both
phenomena and substance, and comprehends conditions, principles and causes underlying all visible
things. It is true that, while in the flesh, the
lower faculties supply much of the material upon
which the Reason acts; still it is the latter that
stamps man as spirit. *The Sense* has its knowledge
through *sensation*, *the Understanding* proceeds *dis-
cursively*, but the Reason knows *intuitively*. Following are at least some of Reason's ideas: Time,
Space, Being and Identity, the True, the Beautiful
and the Good, and the Absolute, or God. These
are the fields of knowledge which place us in rela-

tion with God. I am, therefore, prepared to remark that the faculty of Reason in man is the exact
reproduction of infinite Reason. Surely, however,
while there is no difference in the character of the
functions of infinite Reason and finite Reason, there
is infinite difference in development. God is and
always will be *infinite.* Man is and always will be
finite. Man's knowledge is and always will continue to be *limited—he will forever be a disciple.*
God is omniscient—and will forever be the Teacher.
But were it not for man's intellectual " image of
God," it would never be possible for him to be a
disciple, nor for God to be the Teacher. To be a
learner at the Divine feet, implies divine faculties
in the soul.

Answering to the Reason in the Intellect, there
are emotions in the Susceptibility. These are the
Rational and Spiritual Susceptibilities, to which I
alluded some time ago.

The ideas of the Reason naturally and necessarily
awaken feelings in the heart. In order to illustrate, I call your attention to the following: The
Reason apprehends a rule of right, and the moment that rule is seen, an emotion springs forth in
appeal that the right prevail. Now this feeling
may be termed conscience, which always addresses

its owner: "*Do thy duty.*" Again, in the things
that are made, Reason sees the "eternal power
and Godhead" of the Maker. Such recognition
of Jehovah occasions certain peculiar emotions.
There will be feelings of helplessness and dependence, awe and reverence, faith and love,
worship and praise. Remember, I speak of man
as he was originally created, and not as we now
find him.

It may be meet to say here that the foregoing
emotions are merely given as illustrations, and
while complete as far as they go, they are by no
means all that may be found in the Rational Susceptibility. Some writers mention scientific and
æsthetic emotions as belonging here.

In the matter of the Spiritual Susceptibility, a
few words will suffice. Man, as we have so far
seen him, together with Will in Liberty, of which
some remarks presently, is more than a *thing—he is
a person. Personality involves character, and
character implies a radical spiritual disposition.*
The Spiritual Susceptibility answers to this disposition, and all the individual emotions therein are
governed by this disposition. If a man's disposition is evil, all the feelings in this susceptibility
are evil; if good, then the feelings are good.

Hence, while the Susceptibility itself is permanent,
the emotions are contingent—for as the character
is, so are the emotions, good or evil. If now, in
view of what I have said, the question be asked,
"Do you think that all these feelings which you
have mentioned as belonging originally to man,
do also pervade the heart of God?" I answer,
No, not all. Some do, such as love, and perhaps
others of which we have no knowledge; but others
do not, such as awe, reverence, and so on. The
reason for this is patent. God and man do not
sustain the same relations to each other. One is
Creator, the other creature—one infinite, the other
finite—and this makes a world of difference.

Father and son have identical mental endowments. The relations which they hold to each
other *as father* and *son*, causes a wide divergence of
emotions. While the father has probably more
love for the son, the son surely has more *reverence
for the father*, etc., etc.

Now apply this reasoning to the subject in hand,
and it will be found that my proposition is established, namely, that the disparity of emotion in the
heart of God and man, does not indicate disparity
of constitutions, but only of relations. "So God
created man in His own image."

One thing more. God has, and so has man, Will in Liberty.

The true conception of Will in Liberty involves three things. First, a real alternative in reference to which the spirit is to act. Secondly, the power of electing one of these alternatives rather than another. Thirdly, the power of originating agency to secure that which has been elected. Thus we have *alternative, choice* and *execution.* The process is something like this:—The "flesh," (St. Paul) usually in its own interest, proposes an end to the Will. "The spirit" (St. Paul) also proposes an end, in its own interest and God's glory, to the Will. Now it is competent for the Will to choose the one and leave the other. This done, the Will now goes out in executive act toward the end chosen. In all this man stands infinitely above the brute, and so far as capacity is concerned, *is on a level with God.*

It is valid to say that God does not need occasions for such exercise of Will in Liberty, in order to perfect His nature, *and man does;* but this fact does not argue against God's having such capacity. "So God created man in His own image."

In the foregoing remarks I have outlined to you what I consider the deepest meaning of the Scripture just quoted.

If I have succeeded in making myself understood, I feel reasonably certain that at least many
of you have such an insight into an interesting
and important subject as you have never enjoyed
before.

I now beg leave to briefly indicate two other
aspects, in which it may be said that man is made
in his Maker's likeness.

The truth is, what I have already said fully implies what follows; at the same time I feel to make
particular mention of them for the sake of emphasis.

*Man has in him Gods "image" in respect to
holiness.*

Is Jehovah exempt from all sin and evil? So
was man. Does God love the *true*, the *beautiful*
and the *good?* So did man. *In fine, as in the
Creator, so was the creature.*

Indeed, the truthfulness of this statement is
apparent in the light of what has been said in reference to the soul-structure of man. He being
endowed with a rational nature, after the image of
God—which nature occupying the throne of his
being, ruling and guiding his lower nature, holding it in subjection and abeyance—how could it be
otherwise than that he should be holy, pure and
God-like?

It follows naturally from his moral and spiritual status, just indicated, that man was after the "image of God" in respect to *happiness and love.* It is impossible for the mind to conceive a perfect being without these emotions. They are really elements that necessarily belong to and help to round out and complete perfection. *God must, therefore, possess them, and so also man, by virtue of his very nature.*

In view of what has been advanced in the foregoing observations, we may well see why man is the "lord of creation" ˪and a real son of God. "Let us follow on to know" more of his history and destiny.

LECTURE II.

THE FALL.

GEN. iii. 6.

Gen. iii. 6. She took of the fruit thereof and did eat, and gave also to her husband with her and he did eat.

LECTURE II.

It is simply and alone in the interest of a sad truth that I pen some thoughts on the subject of The Fall.

That such a noble and exalted creature as man should fall away from his all-wise and infinitely loving Maker, is a fact so dark and direful that no one can speak of it with a light and and cheeeful heart; and were it not for the ultimate result, even salvation, to which this discussion may lead, I would fain remain silent.

That man was created in the image of God, and that that image is now in part lost, are two truths that stand as fast as Gibraltar.

The questions, Why? How? To what extent? etc., naturally come up for answer, and in órder to give an answer, I will endeavor to speak under the three heads: *God's law*, *man's transgression*, *the result*.

1. *God's Law.* The question is sometimes put, "If man was all that you ascribe to him, why was a law for his government necessary? I answer,

there are two reasons. First, God being the creator, was also compelled to be ruler. Secondly, It
does not matter how pure a being may be, there
needs to be a law for his guidance and government.
Barbarians have few or no laws, but highly civil-
ized and socially organized nations need many
laws.

In heaven, where all are pure and unspotted,
God's will is law—cheerfully done, but doubtless
that will goes out in different directions, expressed
in various forms; and so in this view, there are
many laws for the conduct of the angelic hosts.
In the preceding lecture I observed that man is
finite, but God infinite; man is disciple, and God,
teacher. I insisted that "the image of God" signifies likeness of rational and spiritual functions, but
by no means equality in development.

Now in the light of this statement, it follows inevitably that to the end of man's development and
training, involving, of course, moral trial and probation, it behooves God to promulgate and teach
His will—*law.* Surely it matters not whether
that law is arbitrary, or adapted to man's physical
or moral nature; all that can be required is that it
be the ruler's voice. This being established, the
subject has no option—*he ought to obey.*

In the matter of the law given to Adam and Eve in Eden, there are many who hold that the forbidden fruit was actually poisonous to the physical body, and that, in so far at least, it was not an arbitrary command, but the opposite.

Others have made an effort to teach that this whole account is nothing but an abstract truth put into a concrete form; an ideal picture set in a material frame; and that, therefore, there was no Eden, nor tree, nor fruit, nor serpent, etc. For myself I believe that such interpretation of holy writ, while it may go under the name of criticism, is destructive and paralyzing, and that it can not be fraught with good results. I prefer to hold on to the literal meaning of Moses' "form of sound words." If, however, any of you can take any comfort from this emasculating style of interpretation, you are welcome to it; and I want to say, moreover, that it does not affect the proposition that God's will, promulgated in any form or manner, is law, and that such law was essential to the spiritual training of the first human pair.

In this connection it may not be without avail to say something further relative to the law in Eden. In the first place, *it was simple and plain.* "The Lord God commanded man, saying, Of every tree of the garden thou mayest freely eat, but of the tree of the knowledge of good and evil thou mayest not eat, for in the day thou eatest thereof thou shalt surely die."

Secondly, *it was easy and practicable.* There was no possible need for this fruit. Their Maker had kindly given all the rest. All their wants were met—all their needs gratified. God had reserved only this one fruit, by which, you see, He expressed His will—a law. They had, as you remember from all I established in the first address, *absolute ability to obey.* Here was a test, to be sure; the animal nature proposing an object to the will, but the spirit also, in the form of its own spiritual worthiness and the honor of Jehovah. Here is a true alternative. The Will in Liberty is regnant, and has the power to choose and enact the latter and reject the former.

Thirdly, *it expressed, in the most positive manner, the Lawgiver's love for the good and hatred of evil.* This deserves more than a passing notice. This very matter has been with many the stone of stumbling and the rock of offence.

It is asked with a great degree of vehemence, and with an air of triumph, if God is all-wise, and knew that Adam and Eve would surely transgress his law, why did He attach to it a heavy and fearful

penalty, namely, *death?* The answer is present.
This is the only possible way there is for showing
His own position respecting holiness on the one
hand, and sin on the other. We see at a glance that
had God been unconcerned as to whether His creatures remained pure or committed sin, the penalty
of the given law would have been mild and small;
but being greatly solicitous, as He was, the sanction
must necessarily be heavy and severe. In fine, the
penalty must be an exact expression of the Lawgiver's character and feeling in regard to holiness,
and its opposite. For be it remembered that the
law was not given to be *broken*, but to be *kept.*
Now this fact involves the additional fact that this
law, with this heavy penalty, wrapped up within its
terms an equally great and precious promise,
namely, *life.* As there was death by eating, so
also there was life by abstaining—and touching
which they could be absolutely certain, inasmuch
as they already possessed the latter.

In this view of it we clearly see that the law
given to Adam and Eve was precisely suited to the
exigency of all the circumstances; and in this, as
in all other things, we observe the love and goodness of God in his dealings with his subjects.

I now pass on to man's transgression.

4

II. *The Transgression.*—The transgression of the holy and righteous law of God by our first parents was naturally preceded by temptation. We examine the account at Gen. iii. 1–5, and find that this fact is plainly set forth in this language: "Now the serpent was more subtile than any beast of the field which the Lord God had made. And he said unto the woman, Yea, hath God said, ye shall not eat of every tree of the garden? The woman said, We may eat of the fruit of the trees of the garden, but of the fruit of the tree which is in the midst of the garden God hath said, Ye shall not eat of it, neither shall ye touch it lest ye die. The serpent said unto the woman, Ye shall not surely die. For God doth know that in the day ye eat thereof then your eyes shall be opened, and ye shall be as gods, knowing good and evil."

Now this narrative attracts our attention to the source and manner of the temptation.

Touching the visible agent—the serpent—it is proper to say there has always prevailed a difference of opinion among the wise. Some maintain that Satan presented himself in the form of a serpent, and that consequently what was seen and heard was not a literal serpent, but the literal devil. Again, there are many who hold that while it was a real serpent which was visible, Satan, invisible, delivered the speech, and of course enacted the beguiling work.

This, I submit, is one of the many things concerning which "we see through a glass darkly," but which we will likely "know even as we are known" in the "sweet bye and bye."

Nor does this lack of knowledge seriously affect us. Of one matter we are certain, and that is, that the "old serpent, the devil"—in *any* way or manner, but surely in *some* way or manner—accomplished his designs, and brought about the most direful catastrophe the earth has ever witnessed. I take it to be interesting to many of you to give the opinion of a few learned theologians as to the *modus operandi* of the temptation which led to the fall. Dr. Knapp states his opinion thus: "Eve sees the serpent on the forbidden tree, and probably eating of the fruit, and yet no harm follows. She sees, on the contrary, that the serpent is very active and knowing. She reasons thus: 'The tree cannot be injurious; the command cannot be meant in earnest.' The serpent seems to say to her, "Consider how vigorous and wise I am—you will not die, you will become wise.' And Eve now thinks as God is the only being wiser than herself, she would become wise like God. Thus at length she ate of the tree."

Drs. Storr and Flatt's explanation: "The natural serpent ate of the forbidden fruit, and Eve observes it. The devil takes advantage of this circumstance, presents himself, and, though invisible to Eve, carries on a conversation with her for the purpose of inducing her to transgress the command of God. Eve, not seeing the devil, supposed it was the serpent that spoke to her. Having known the serpent before, and never having discovered in it' the gift of rational conversation, Eve naturally concluded that the eating of the forbidden fruit had conferred the gift upon her."

Another circumstance of the temptation is this, that Satan appeared first to the woman.

This fact is usually accounted for on the assumption that Eve, and all women ever since, was the weaker vessel morally, and that the ingenuity of the devil led him, as a matter of course, to inveigle her first, and thus gradually work his way up to the stronger—*good and superior Adam.* I do not agree to this. I do not agree, because I believe facts point to the reverse of the above. How any one can postulate that woman is the weaker, morally and spiritually, I for one can not conceive, inasmuch as all history and, I think, psychology, "*sound her praise abroad.*"

I believe in the total depravity of both sexes since the fall, but this does not blind me to the undisputed fact that woman is clearly more susceptible to spiritual influences and truths than man. As a witness to this statement, I cite that seventy-five per cent. of the disciples of Christ to-day are women. But the voice of history is not the only voice in her favor. I am absolutely certain that a psychological investigation, if it could be conducted, would establish the truth of a greater spiritual and a lesser animal element in the feminine, than in the opposite sex. If this be true now, I am sure it was pre-eminently true before "sin and death entered into the world."

My judgment, therefore, is, in view of what I have observed above, that Satan attacked Eve first because he was sagacious enough to know that if he succeeded in his wiles with her, being the stronger, he would have easy and short work with Adam. Eve was the key to the situation. *Let Petersburg fall, and Richmond is a foregone conclusion. Let Eve disobey, and Adam is certain to yield.* Now let Moses speak: "She took the fruit thereof and did eat, and gave also to her husband,

with her, and he did eat.'' In this we find not the
slightest hesitation or resistance on the part of
Adam. I have spoken somewhat at length on the
foregoing, for the sole reason of vindicating woman
from the aspersion so often heaped upon her by the
other sex—from whom we have a right to look for
better things.

Relative to the time when the fall took place it
is impossible to venture more than a surmise.
Many, however, are of the opinion that it took
place on the first day of their occupancy of Paradise. This may be true or it may not be true—who
knows? But one thing is certain, which I will
make more evident later on, namely, that it did oc-
cur before the conception of their first-born child.

Before advancing to the third part of this discussion, I desire to share your indulgence a brief period
on the *moral evils* involved in the *transgression.*
This I do not so much in the interest of mere intellectual edification as in that of moral improvement.

First, *there was a sad display of ingratitude.*
The spirit of thankfulness should always have a
large place in every living bosom. It should heave
the breast and dominate both tongue and life.
This is peculiarly true of the occupants of glorious
Eden. In their own personality, as well as in every

environment, there existed not only a reflection, but a true counterpart of God and heaven. They surely had no right to wish for anything more. The spirit yielding to the flesh already at the very beginning of the temptation, at least to some extent, quieted the voice of thanksgiving, and gave room to a spirit of discontent. How sad to contemplate, but yet how true! Moreover, this same devil too often rules in our moral empire within, and disallows one of the leading principles and activities of the soul—gratitude, grateful praise!

Secondly. *Here is pride.* That Adam and Eve should have a high and noble opinion of themselves is not incompatible with moral purity. To remember appreciatingly their origin and present standing was a holy duty and an exalted privilege. In this view of it we observe the consistency of a "lofty spirit." When, however, this legitimate notion became contaminated with the desires of the "flesh," it remained no longer pure and proper, but became selfish and sinful, and the expression and outgoing thereof led to iniquity and rebellion, inasmuch as it lifted the creature above the Creator. Gen. iii. 6.

Thirdly. *We notice here a display of great credulity, and yet great unbelief. Faith in the word*

*of the Maker, and distrust of the fabrication of
Satan, is the natural order. This order was reversed.*

Now I wish to say right here that it was decidedly
easier to follow the right order, for that was the
God-ordained one. The current of Adam and Eve's
life ran that way. Trust in God and disbelief in
Satan was in accordance with the constitution of
their soul. One was natural, the other unnatural.
Notwithstanding, they held the lever in their own
hand. In the very nature of the case it remained
for them to say whether they will go forward or
backward. They decided. The reverse lever of
their life was pulled. *They ran backward and
wrecked!*

Alas and alas! that millions on millions of intelligent people should commit the same inexcusable
folly in this late day, when the appeal of God and
man is loud and strong to choose a "more excellent
way."

With feelings of sadness we now approach the
result of the transgression.

III. *The Result.*—For the purpose of preparing
the way for what I consider as the direct and positive consequence of the transgression, I give those
which are incidental first. In this we are guided
by the narration in Gen. iii.

At the seventh verse we read: "And the eyes of them both were opened, and they knew that they were naked, and they sewed fig leaves together and made themselves aprons." This intimates something of the unspeakable fear and shame that overwhelmed Adam and Eve.

Before this nothing but joy and peace thrilled their souls. Holy innocence, as that of angels, sheathed their persons. Now they are bowed down with shame, and their grief is more than they can bear. Satan's words are fulfilled: "That in the day ye eat thereof, then your eyes shall be opened, and ye shall be as gods (not God, but gods, that is, devils), knowing good and evil." They obtained "knowledge," they became "wise," but it was the "knowledge" and "wisdom" of Diabolus; and the tribute which they paid for their learning was nothing less than their happy, pure and peaceful innocence, yea, even their own life, as indeed also the life of all humanity. Read verse 8.

At the ninth to the thirteenth verse we find a record of the manner in which God took the offenders to task, and their heart-broken confession. It is not at all possible for us even to imagine the pang and terror which must have seized, tiger-like, upon their souls, and especially so as they listened to

the sentence of punishment their Ruler pronounced upon them. Read the 16–19 verses.

As I said before, these results are only incidental and concomitant. They are the things
that come to the surface of their life. If this were
the major portion of their calamity, it were sad
enough, it is true; but being, as it is, only the
minor portion, what can be thought and said of
the other?

We remember that the sanction of the law was
"death," in transgression. Now "death" is a
term that may apply variously. It is a relative
term, for a thing may not be absolutely "dead,"
when yet it is so called in comparison with something that has more "life," or different "life."
Thus, for example, a plant is not "dead," but still
it has not the mental "life" of an animal, and
hence in a comparison it is sometimes called
"dead." An animal has "life," but compared
with the soul "life" of man, it fades so far into
the back-ground that it is pronounced "dead."
It is also true that neither of these lower creatures
can lift itself into the next higher realm of
"life."

Applying this scientific truth to the subject in
hand, we plainly see that God, pronouncing

"death" upon Adam and Eve, did not mean that they should become instantly lifeless, as that word is commonly understood. Hereby do we cut the Gordian knot that presents itself so often to many people touching this very thing.

Many good, truth-loving folk cannot understand how a truthful God could say that "death" should ensue disobedience, but death did not follow— for Adam and Eve continued to live many hundred years after. From this fact, together with what I said in the preceding paragraph, we cannot but believe that the penalty of "death" did not apply chiefly, if at all, to the physical nature of those to whom it was given.

I feel to aver, however, as guarding the foregoing sentence, that it surely is reasonable to suppose that the seeds of death, as we now know it, were sown in the fall. We know absolutely nothing of what would have been if there had been no transgression. There might have been a gradual transformation of the physical into the spiritual, running through hundreds and perhaps thousands of years, thus fitting and adjusting man to a heavenly existence. Or the change might have occurred "as in the twinkling of an eye," like unto that promised to the righteous at the last day—or

in any of the thousand ways open to the infinite
Creator. One thing only seems certain, and that
is, that our body and soul would not have been
disunited through disease, pain and sorrow, and
the body left to decompose in the grave. Inasmuch, however, as God said, "In the day"—that
very day—"that thou eatest thereof thou shalt
die;" and inasmuch as Adam and Eve did not
physically die "in that day," we are drawn to conclude that the term "death" does not primarily
apply to the body. The only other alternative is
the soul. We conclude, accordingly, that the penalty of the law fell on the intellectual, moral and
spiritual natures of man — spiritual and eternal
"death."

What I have to say further I will arrange under
two topics: Original Sin, and Natural Depravity.

Original Sin, properly speaking, is simply the
commission of the first sin, which in its outer form
was the eating of the fruit of the "tree of the
knowledge of God and evil," but in its inner spirit,
was the disobedience of God's plain and simple
word, or law.

I will, if you please, for the sake of an easier understanding of the subject, range under this head
the whole result of the fall as it affected Adam and
Eve.

In the first lecture I tried to point out the difference existing between man's lower, or animal, and
higher, or rational, natures. In the light of what I
then said it is patent to us all that the rational nature, in virtue of which man was made in the
"image of God," was designed to reign over the
"flesh." This it was easy for the rational nature
to do, for it was created for the throne, *and therefore inherited both authority and power to reign.*
Strange and incredible as it may seem to us, when
the competition between the sense and spirit was
ushered in, the spirit abdicated, and the sense
usurped, the throne. This, we observe, inverted
the order of their constitution, and reversed the
entire outflow of their being.

But some one may here ask, "Is then, in view of
of what you said, the inferior nature of man essen-
tially and inherently evil?" I answer, No, by no
means. Such a postulate would involve the Maker
in the creating of something that was not "good."

I remarked some time ago that this is the very
nature that fits man for life and activity on the
earth. Indeed, so far as we can see, it is absolutely
indispensable to our earthly existence. From this
we conclude that as it came from God's hand it
was just as pure and perfect *in its realm,* as the

superior nature was *in its higher realm.* The
point that we must bear in mind lies here, that the
carnal functions were designed as servants and not
as masters,—*subjects and not rulers.* Destined to
be mortal and temporal, how is it possible for it to
direct and govern the immortal and eternal spirit?
This is precisely what it began to do after the fall,
and what it has continued to do ever since, in all
who are not "born again" by the spirit of God.

*In this inversion and disturbance of the natures
in man consists the source and fountain of all actual
sin.*

*This also constitutes the all-sufficient reason for
exclusion from heaven and consignment to hell.*

I am firm in my belief that the principal result
of the disobedience in Eden was subjective, con-
sisting chiefly in the things foregoing. At the
same time I am also persuaded that there was an
objective consequence—objective I say, namely, in
the mind of God. Jehovah's law to Adam and
Eve was expressive of his perfections. Now when
they transgressed they offended these attributes.
They offended them in the sense that it was not
possible for a truthful and holy, therefore just, God
to continue "life" when he had threatened "death"
in the event of transgression. In point of time it

is evident that this objective result came first. Afterwards, and by the direct fiat of God, came the subjective. I have no faith myself in the theory that any disturbance or poisoning resulted from the mere eating of the forbidden fruit. In view of what has been just said, it is quite manifest that man turned away from God, and that God turned away from man—in some sense.

This, then, is the condition of things immediately after the fall. The Lawgiver's offended perfections; spiritual "death" of the soul, which involves, *privatively* (1) "A want of the fear of God and of confidence toward him, and also a want of holiness;" (2) "a deficiency of the powers requisite for attaining holiness by man's own exertion ; and *positively*, sinful propensities, viz., a preponderance of carnal powers over reason, as also shame and sorrow."

I now proceed to the consideration of natural depravity.

Why and how was the sin of Adam and Eve transmitted to their descendants? is a question somewhat anxiously asked. Many answers have been returned by the learned. Augustine held that all the posterity of Adam were, in the most literal sense, already in him, and that Adam's sin

is, therefore, most justly imputed to all his posterity. A second explanation is that "Adam was
not only the natural or seminal, but also the moral
and federal head of the whole human race, and,
accordingly, that the sin of Adam is imputed on
the same principle on which the doings of the head
of a family, or of the plenopotentiary of a state, are
imputed to his family or state, although they had
no personal agency in his doings." A third
theory deduces the doctrine of imputation from
God's foreknowledge of what is conditionally possible, and which is termed the "Scientia Media"
of God. This means, in plain words, that God
foresaw that each one of us, if placed in Adam's
circumstances, would have done just as he did,
would have been guilty of the same sin ; therefore,
God imputes Adam's sin to us.

I deem that the foregoing theories are sufficient
in number to show the drift of philosophical
thought on this subject. I am sure that if any of
my readers feel to adopt either of these explanations as their own, I shall not say a word to hinder
them, although personally I reject all as totally
unsatisfactory.

For myself, I do not believe in a direct Divine
"imputation" at all—I mean an arbitrary imputa-

tion. God caused this moral evil to be transmitted according to the laws in our constitution,
and that, I hold, is all there is of it. I feel that if
I should interpret anything more into this truth,
I should evince a more than ordinary amount of
inborn or "imputed" depravity! But who will
say that this is not enough? Let us recount what
it involves. This depravity works God's displeasure against us, alienates us from Him, occasions
and causes all overt and actual sins, shuts us out
of heaven, and casts us into hell. Of course it destroys all our peace, and fills our breast with unceasing woe.

> "Sorrow tracketh wrong,
> As echo follows song,
> On, on, on."

This, then, is the sad and distressing condition
of all men since the fall, in view of which we may
well say with the apostle Paul, "Who shall deliver
us from the body of this death? I thank God
through our Lord Jesus Christ."

> "Lord I would spread my sore distress
> And guilt before Thine eyes;
> Against Thy laws, against Thy grace,
> How high my crimes arise.

5

"I from the stock of Adam came,
    Unholy and unclean ;
All my original is shame,
    And all my nature sin.

"Cleanse me, O Lord, and cheer my soul
    With Thy forgiving love ;
Oh, make my broken spirit whole,
    And bid my pains remove.

"Let not Thy Spirit e'er depart,
    Nor drive me from Thy face;
Create anew my sinful heart,
    And fill it with Thy grace."

LECTURE III.

PROMISE OF A DELIVERER. CALL OF ABRAM.
GOD'S DEALING WITH THE ISRAELITES.

GEN. iii. 15.

Gen. iii. *15.* I will put enmity between thee and the woman, and between thy seed and her seed; it shall bruise thy head, and thou shalt bruise his heel.

LECTURE III.

I THANK God most devoutly that in this word of promise we are led from under the cloud of sin and shame and woe into the light of free grace and a glorious salvation.

Although man had no right to look for the gracious interposition of his Lord and Master, still, knowing, as we do, that "God is love," we may see that such would likely be the case. Indeed, I say reverently, that viewing the perfection, yea the fatherhood, of God, in the light of Christianity, we are compelled to assert that He must—that He must if there be a possible plan by which it can be accomplished—redeem us once more.

The above remark is not intended to convey the idea that what we now see and know, or think we see and know, was also clearly understood by Adam and Eve. I do not believe that they enjoyed any such hopeful anticipations. They had heard the word of doom, and accepted that as their final destiny.

(61)

Now in this view of their condition we can not possibly imagine the thrill of joy that darted through their being as they listened to the hope-inspiring promise of a Redeemer for them and for the race—one who should crush the serpent's head. To Eve there must have been a double joy in this announcement; for it meant the crushing of him who had caused her to fall, and that this should be achieved by the "seed of the woman," implying, as it did, that she herself should contribute to this triumphant consummation.

Suffice it to say that while our first parents understood but very little about the plan of redemption then and there promised, they did know enough to quicken faith in the love and power of their Maker, that in a suitable way the race of men should be recovered to God. This faith sufficed to reciprocate God's love to them, and they henceforth lived in affectionate obedience to him. I beg leave to state in this connection that in the lecture —Mediatorial Work of Christ—some more light will be thrown on this topic, that I do not feel justified to anticipate here. A word more, however, may profitably be spoken relative to a foregoing remark. In view of what I averred touching the moral recovery of Adam and Eve, the question

may be put, "Does not such recovery involve all
that they lost? and why, therefore, should their
offspring be depraved, seeing that the parents were
"born again" before the conception of the first
born? My answer is, This question assumes
more than can be proved. It is by no means
certain just at what juncture in the history of Adam
and Eve this promise was given. It is true that it
probably took place very soon after the Fall, but
yet that does by no means argue against the sup-
position that Cain was already conceived, and that
the depravity of the parents was transmitted to his
nature. A second answer may appear in this form,
that although the pardon and restoration of Adam
and Eve may have taken place instantly after their
spiritual lapse, it did not bring them back to the
precise status which they enjoyed before such lapse.
Philosophically speaking, it is true that their two
distinct natures, which, so to speak, had changed
places, the flesh becoming regnant and the spirit
servant, in the Fall, had been restored to their
proper places ; at the same time it is easy to conceive that there was left, as the ravages of disobedience, a signal insubordination of the flesh.
The former once humiliated and the latter once'
exalted, betokens and prophesies an evil that can

only be overcome by the power of Divine Grace.
Just why this should be, may never be very evident
in the "nature of the case." It is properly
relegated to the arcana of the Absolute. It is,
however, a proper matter for belief that all this
should be so, "for so it seemed good in His sight,"
in order to bring the highest good to the race, and
the most splendid glory to His own wisdom, power
and grace. Of one thing we are absolutely certain : that Cain, supposably the first born, was
desperately wicked, the germ or tendency of which
was an inheritance ; and that all men from him
down to the child just born are not one whit
better. This fact is stronger than any and all
opposing theories that have ever been "evolved
out of the inner consiousness" of philosophers.

But we turn back to the promise. In its light
we can say that God has turned in favor unto man,
for the sake and because of the prospective work
and merits of the "Seed of the Woman." So also
may Adam and Eve not only, but all men everywhere, "repent and believe" and turn lovingly
unto God, by the help and grace offered them
by Him who "shall bruise the serpent's head."
My conviction is, that Adam and Eve accepted
the proffered help and are saved ; Cain refused it

and was cursed. Abel and Seth accepted and were good and holy men; and as for the rest of the family we know nothing, although we may conjecture that some were saved and others lost.

The Scriptures teach us that in the line of Seth were many holy men, one of whom never saw death, and it is said, "He was not, for God took him." As the ages rolled by the people waxed worse and worse. In the course of 1600 years after the creation, "God saw that the wickedness of man was great in the earth, and that every imagination of the thought of his heart was only evil continually."

"But Noah found grace in the sight of the Lord." "Noah was a just man, and perfect in his generation, and Noah walked with God." The blotting out of man by the great "Catastrophe," the deluge, next ensued. Noah and his wife, with his three sons and their wives, constituted the remnant of the human race after the flood subsided. These eight persons were the nucleus of new nations of men. God renewed with a sign the great and precious promises of His favor upon all humanity. A new spiritual seed was again planted in the earth. Another opportunity was granted, and another effort was made, to im-

part a heavenward impulse to the coming generations. This for two reasons : first, for the immediate weal of those ages ; and secondly, for the
purpose of hastening the "fulness of time" for
the advent of the " Seed of the woman."

But the oncoming generation were wayside
ground. They gathered rocks upon their soil, so
that the seed could not germinate and bring forth
grain. The impulse imparted was resisted, and
the nations, as before the flood, instead of *upward*
went *downward*, so that there were but few who
had the fear of the Lord before their eyes. The
exigency of the times and the character of God's
plan of redemption, demanded that a new and
superior method should be originated and introduced, by which to prepare the world for the
promised Redeemer.

THE CALL OF ABRAM.

Abram, afterward named Abraham, was a native
of Ur of the Chaldees (Gen. xv. 7; Acts vii. 2 and
3). After the first call fell on his ear, and in obedience thereto, he, with his father's family, traveled toward Canaan, the place of his future home,
according to promise; sojourning at Haran for a
certain period of time. Here the Lord called the

second time, and again Abram responded, this time under the special guidance of Providence, completing his journey to a "land I will shew thee"—named above.

Critics have tried their best to discredit the historic existence of this sublime Old Testament character, but resulting chiefly in discrediting their own critical acumen, and personal piety and reverence. Dozy, a great Arabic scholar of Leyden, declares that "Abraham was originally the name of a stone-fetish, and Sarah the name of a hollow in which it was placed." Another scholar, Goldziher, says: "Abraham was originally the starry sky divinely worshiped." Still other critics aver that Abraham, Isaac and Jacob were gods of the old Hebrew Pantheon. I give these instances from among many others, as illustrative of the length to which men go to overthrow the record of the Holy Scriptures, and at the same time to show how they antagonize and refute each other. When Satan assumes the role of critic he always makes bad work of it, for he is at home anywhere but in the Bible. One of the best arguments for *Christ* is *Christianity;* the best argument for the personal existence of *Abraham* is the *Hebrew race.* That race now exists and has existed for upwards of

four thousand years. It must be accounted for,
but how can it be without a head, an organizer, so
to speak? And pray why shall we throw away
the record of its origin in the Scriptures, at least
before we have a better one? Now Moses, the inspired historian, writes plainly and deliberately,
that the head and organizer of the Hebrew race is
Abraham. *I accept the record as literal and bona
fide, and reject all opposing theories.*

If the question should arise, why was it necessary
for God to call Abraham away from his country
and friends and family into Canaan, a place which
he knew not?—a twofold answer may be ventured.

First—It may have been necessary in order that
he might be made solely dependent on a higher
wisdom and power and authority than any earthly.
Abraham's family and friends and country were
idolatrous. Both his moral inheritance and en-
vironments were evil and evil only. "Evil communications corrupt good manners." Humanly
speaking, it would have been morally impossible to
train Abraham for his life mission among such surroundings. The wicked influences pressing upon
him from every side would have proved too much
for him. "But nothing is impossible with God,"
you say. That is true; still God does not usually

develop His purpose on the earth without all reasonable precautions. God is not prodigal with His
miraculous powers. For, reading the narrative of
His interpositions for man, one is impressed with
the fact that between the exercise of ordinary pre-
caution and miraculous power, the All-wise and
Almighty generally chooses the former.

It is plainly evident, therefore, for reasons
stated above, that Abraham would likely be commanded to forsake "all" in Haran, to follow the
Lord whither He would lead him.

It cannot be denied that the inhabitants of Canaan were just as wicked as those of Chaldea.
What advantage accrued to Abraham by shifting
him out of "the pan into the fire?" Much every
way. He was separated from his friends and asso-
ciates and surroundings, whom he touched daily,
to live in a comparatively isolated condition. Although in his new home he saw idolatry and many
other abominations, he did not so directly come
in contact with them. He was much freer from
"evil communications." Again, this very separation and isolation threw him more directly and
voluntarily on the help of God. He sought not
the vain help of man, but the power and guidance
of Jehovah.

Second—Another reason likely lies in the fact of the favorable location of Canaan. Canaan takes its name from "Canaan, the youngest son of Ham, and grandson of Noah, who settled here after the confusion of tongues at Babel, and divided the country among his.eleven sons, each of whom became the head of numerous tribes, that ultimately became a distinct nation." This country is also known by various other names: The Land of Israel, The Land of Jehovah, The Land of Promise, The Holy Land, The Land of Judah, and Palestine; some passages in Scripture refer to it as "Earth" and the "Land," likely in view of its location and character. It measures about two hundred miles North and South by eighty to one hundred miles East and West. It comprises within its borders the greatest variety of climate, and splendid fertility of soil—"a land flowing with milk and honey." By virtue of mountains, and waters and deserts around, it serves as a natural refuge to its inhabitants, protecting largely from hostile invasions. Moreover, the very soil and climate and scenery was adapted to inspire and foster a lively and healthy religious sentiment and activity. In fine, it was *the spot*, infinitely above any other, destined from eternity to become the cradle of an "elect people." In the light of these facts, I do not hesitate to say that we find here a complete justification of Abraham's call into Canaan.

Abraham, under the leading of Providence, settled in Shechem. The promise went forth from God that "in Abraham and his seed shall all the nations of the earth be blessed." This language, doubtless, had reference to succeeding generations of men all over the earth, but special reference to Christ and Christianity.

In point of fact, this is exactly what has been, and now is, the case. Generally speaking, wherever the Hebrew race came in contact with other nations, some blessing was left behind ; and in the most absolute sense, wherein Christ in Christianity touches, *a most benign and exalting effect is produced.*

The promise reads "To thee and thy seed."

Now the immediate seed of Abraham was Isaac, and the seed of Isaac was Jacob, and the seed of Jacob was the twelve patriarchs—I allude to the line of promise and decree of God—and the twelve patriarchs were the fountain heads of the twelve tribes. Up to this time there are only individual Hebrews, and as yet no Nation. But God's plan for the world's redemption involves not a few only,

but many,—even many hundred years before the
Saviour's advent in the flesh,—and this for several
reasons. First, *individuals* might withstand all
the evil influences crowding upon them from their
surroundings, but not half so well as when encouraged and supported by *national* life ; secondly,
individuals might do something in the way of promoting the knowledge of God and true worship of
Him, but a *nation* can do infinitely more. *Individuals* might have and make use of rites, ordinances and ceremonies for their moral and
spiritual edification and upbuilding, but a *collec-
tion of individuals*, bound together into an organic
unit, can make incalculably better use of them.
From these premises we naturally conclude that the
seed of Abraham will not only be like the "sand
of the sea-shore" and the "stars of the sky" for
number, but also that these *many* will be *one nation*. "E Pluribus Unum." "In union there is
strength." This one great and mighty nation, in
the most "goodly land" of the wide world, if they
remain in the favor of the infinite Jehovah, will be
proof against all the corruptions and machinations
of the world and the devil. This is not all. Such
will be able to destroy the nations that were
morally "ready to perish," to declare liberty to

the captives among the residue, who were awaiting
the coming of the "Day of Jehovah." This nation will be a savor of life unto life to an untold
multitude, and a savor of death unto death to all
the rest, who had steeled their hearts against the
appeal of Love.

The foregoing observations lead us to see that
the selling of Joseph, one of the patriarchs, into
Egypt; his godly and honorable career in the
court of Pharoah ; the removal of Jacob and his
sons to the same country ; the slavery of the
Hebrews through a number of centuries, during
which time they increased from seventy souls to
upwards of three millions ; their deliverance at the
hand of Moses ; their sojourn in the wilderness and
their final settlement in Palestine, were every one
the filling up of the details of God's plan of redemption for them and for us.

This bondage in Egypt secured not only that
there should be a great increase in numbers, growing out of their mode of life and the influence of
climate, etc., but that, on account of their common
interests, common religion, and common sufferings, they should be insolubly compacted and
united as a people, who reckoned themselves the
children of Abraham, Isaac and Jacob.

6

Their miraculous deliverance through Moses impressed them anew with their littleness and dependence, and God's greatness and love. By this bondage and this deliverace they were disciplined and taught to yield themselves into the mighty hand of God. The detention in the wilderness, although primarily caused by their own moral weakness and cowardice, was a part of God's plan to prepare and equip them for an independent national life. Up to this time the people were not prepared for, and God had not given them, laws and rites and ordinances commensurate with their present and future needs and greatness. But a new epoch in their history is at hand: God takes a great step forward. Fasts and feasts, rites and ordinances, laws and precepts, are proclaimed and established. In the tabernacle, a central place of worship is furnished ; and in the Priesthood, a Mediatorship between the people and God is vouchsafed and warranted. Through these instrumentalities, and during the season of this wilderness life, the Hebrews advanced a thousand cubits in their national life and in the knowledge of God.

It does not avail to say that for all that the Lord had done, the Israelites fell again and again into all sorts of vices and crimes and sins. Is not the same thing true now, with all our nineteenth century light and grace? Why then should we expect more from those people than we do of ourselves—I mean than many among us do. This I say not to justify them, but only to show something of the depth of human depravity then and now. One thing is sure, namely, the Israelites were almost infinitely above the rest of mankind in character and conduct.

At this point of our discussion, it may not be without good results to glance merely at the philosophy of the various Heaven-ordained institutions in the possession of the Hebrews. I have not the time to enter into details, nor does the scope of this lecture demand it; but I shall present the matter merely in a general way, to show that the Lord is a God of wisdom and order.

We take, first, the Priesthood. The setting apart for his holy office, the induction into his office, the garments or robes which he wore, his peculiar and specific function as a priest in the outer court, and in the Holy Place, and the High Priest once a year in the Most Holy Place—all these are powerful factors in teaching the people the holiness, justice and love of God. The same truths were impressed by the various sacrifices and offerings, and the additional fact that God required a yielding of themselves and all theirs to His cause and service. The different feasts and seasons of rejoicing stirred up their memories of God's gracious dealings in the past, and led their minds to His promises for the future, and thus developed a spirit of praise and trust and renewed consecration.

Circumcision was a perpetual reminder of Jehovah's covenant with them through Abraham, Isaac and Jacob, and, of course, also of their dedication to God and of the necessity of cutting away sin and of a life of purity and virtue.

The scape-goat—one slain and the other sent into the wilderness—spoke loudly of atonement and consequent forgiveness and forgetfulness—even to the extent of oblivion—of sins.

The Tabernacle and its service, and the place of God's presence in the Holy of holies, joined in declaring the majesty and perfections of God, and the depravity of man and his absolute need of atonement.

Then there was also an abstract rule of conduct, the Ten Commandments. These magnified the relations between man and God and man and man, and the duties inseparably attached to these relations.

It suffices to observe here that all these tangible and visible ordinances, rites and ceremonies, were calculated to have a most wholesome effect on the Israelites. They conveyed three classes of knowledge: namely, a knowledge of the holiness, justice, love and mercy of God, and His rightful demands upon His people; a knowledge of their awful sinfulness and their inequality to God's requirements; and a knowledge of the advent of a Priest who should make atonement in his own blood, and through whom they should not only have pardon of sin, but also help to live a life of purity and obedience to the commands and precepts of God.

We now take a forward look. We lift up our eyes and behold the promise of God fulfilled. Moses is dead, but Joshua takes his place. The mighty host of Israel takes possession of the "goodly" Canaan. Every step is hotly contested, but under the guidance of Him who laughs in derision at His enemies, their prior rights are established and secured, the land is divided, and the tribes settle in their allotted places.

From this time forward the spectacle presented in the conduct of the Israelites is by no means always pleasant to our vision. Disobedience and idolatry were followed by the judgments of God,

which in turn were succeeded by repentance and a
hearty turning to their offended Ruler. After a
season of peace and unbounded prosperity they
again forgot the Lord and again were punished, or
disciplined, and again they returned to their "first
love."

The history of this nation is so well known that
I refrain entering into details concerning it. But
this one matter I wish firmly to impress, namely,
that in spite of all this very checkered life, in spite
of all these oft defections and lapses, in spite of all
the moral and spiritual deformity which we perceive, there were many, very many, among them
who remained true to the covenant of promise,
and who constituted the "salt of the earth" and
the "light of the world" during those ages. God's
plan for the world was not defeated, but consum-
mated. While many, yes, even the majority of the
Jews refused to accept Christ when He appeared
among them, still, thank the Lord, there were
many who like Zacharias were "devout men," and
who, like Simeon, could say : "Now lettest thou
thy servant to depart in peace, for mine eyes have
seen thy salvation; a light to lighten the Gentiles
and a glory to thy people Israel." More than this.
This leaven which God had placed in Canaan had

more or less leavened the whole lump. Thus it was that at the appearing of the Son of God in Bethlehem's lowly stable, the Magi from the East, guided by a star, came to worship and offer their gold, frankincense and myrrh. For myself, I gladly cherish the belief that "all the nations of the earth were blest" through the "seed of Abraham," as agents in the hand of the triune God, Father, Son, and Holy Ghost. "Lift up your heads, O ye gates, and the King of glory shall come in." This voice, heard and heeded by many among the Jews and Gentiles, accounts for the triumphal march in the earth of "great David's greater Son," from the time of his crucifixion to the present.

I have fulfilled my purpose. I have furnished the link between the Fall of the "first Adam" and the blessed advent of the "second Adam from Heaven."

"In songs of sublime adoration and praise,
    Ye pilgrims for Zion who press,
  Break forth and extol the great Ancient of Days,
    His rich and unmerited grace.

"His love, from eternity, burn'd for our race,
    Broke forth and discover'd its flame;
  And now with the cords of His kindness He draws,
    And brings us to love His great name.

"Oh, had He not pitied the state we were in,
  Our bosoms His love had ne'er felt:
We all would have lived, would have died too in sin,
  And sunk with the load of our guilt.

"What was there in man that could merit esteem,
  Or give the Creator delight?
'Twas "even so, Father," we ever must sing,
  Because it seemed good in Thy sight.

"Urged on by His grace, did the Saviour appear,
  The bearer of help from above:
Now all who are thirsting may freely draw near
  And drink in the streams of His love.

"Then give all the glory to His holy name,
  To Him all the glory belongs;
Be ours the high joys still to sound forth His fame,
  And crown Him in each of our songs."

LECTURE IV.

THE GOD-MAN.

LUKE ii. 7.

Luke ii. 7. "And she brought forth her first-born son, and wrapped him in swaddling-clothes, and laid him in a manger because there was no room for them in the inn."

LECTURE IV.

"Even so, come, Lord Jesus. Amen."

"Thanks be unto God for His unspeakable gift."

"God so loved the world that He gave His only begotten Son, that whosoever believeth on Him should not perish, but have everlasting life."

The question is sometimes asked, was redemption by Jesus Christ the only way by which it was possible to bring men "from death unto life and from the power of Satan unto God?" The answer is, we cannot be absolutely certain. However, on the basis of God's infiniteness we may infer that it was not the only plan. It would at least seem to detract from the wisdom and power of God to conclude otherwise than that it was one plan out of many possible plans. From all that we can know to the contrary, the present scheme may be one of a thousand others available to Him with whom all things are possible. It will not do to argue that we can comprehend redemption through Christ, but that we cannot divine how else it could possibly be accomplished. Now the truth is that be-

(83)

fore the present plan of salvation was revealed to us
in the Scriptures, or apart from such revelation,
the finite mind was not and would not be competent to understand how God can save man at all ;
in fact, even under the light of such revelation
many still cannot see it. So it is that now we do
not know how else we might be ransomed from
sin, but if another plan than the present one had
been elected and revealed by the Lord, I doubt not
that plan would be as easily understood as this one.

Another reason why I infer a plurality of plans
available for man's salvation is this: without it,
avoid it as we may, God is involved in inspiring
and causing the foulest deeds that have ever been
perpetrated on earth, namely, Christ's betrayal,
denial, condemnation and crucifixion—by Judas,
Peter, the Jewish Council and the soldiers—and
each and all directly and indirectly implicated.
For it is plainly evident that to the end that Christ
may redeem us by His blood, some one must shed
that blood, and hence we witness the host of hell
let loose on Him, in the order enumerated above.
Now surely if this was the only method, God must
have decreed and ordained that all this should
come to pass. There was no alternative, and,
therefore, the instruments, or agents, are not to be

blamed and censured for their diabolical work—
they must have been passive and helpless. This
involves the fact that God proceeded on the Jesuit
motto: "The end justifies the means"—or in
what the Apostle Paul terms "doing evil that
good may come."

How does this accord with our settled belief
touching the goodness and love and holiness of
God? The question is a sufficient answer, inasmuch as it implies an utter absurdity. In point of
fact, tens of thousands of good thinking people, of
a philosophical turn of mind, have become hope-
lessly entangled in this matter, and have become
totally lost to Christianity. They assume, and
were perhaps taught, that the established plan of
grace was the only possible one ; and upon this
premise they reasoned out to the logical and inevitable conclusion that God inspired and caused
men to shed innocent blood. From this they
shrink with all the enthusiasm and energy of their
souls, and land perhaps in agnosticism and perhaps in positive atheism.

I am aware of the fact that efforts have been
made to explain this discrepancy in our notion of
the character of God, but certainly without settling
the minds of thinking men. For example, it may

and has been said that all these agents, as Judas,
etc., were wicked men before this tragedy took
place, and therefore all that was needed was to
actuate them to carry out their evil nature in the
commission of this deed, and that not God but the
devil incited them to it. Again, it is said these
people had so sinned before that they had fallen
under the eternal damnation of God ; their destiny
was sealed, and so now God may properly use them
for the furtherance of His gracious plan in behalf
of the world, that whosoever will may be saved.
Now all these explanations do not touch the underlying fact, that God must have decreed that
thus it should be, and that He bent Heaven and
Earth to fulfil this foreordination. Like Banquo's
ghost, the thought will "not down" that God
caused sinful deeds.

I personally rejoice in the firm conviction that to
the mind of God there were many plans by which
he might redeem man. Speaking after the manner of men, I may say that looking down through
the vista of the future, God knew exactly what the
state of society would be from first to last; and not
only this, but also what the moral and spiritual
status and conduct of each individual would be,
from the time of birth to the time of death. Be it

remembered that this knowledge was original, and independent of the activity of His will. In other words, this knowledge guided and determined what His will should choose and ordain, and not the opposite. What he shall choose and do is grounded on His knowledge. In this we differ from those who hold that God's omniscience is the result of foreordination, putting the will first and knowledge second, and thus reversing the order of the mind's capacities—knowing, feeling, and willing—as revealed to us in consciousness.

Following up the statement above made that God knew all things from the beginning, and holding in His mind different plans of redemption, it is easily seen that he may choose and ordain the one He pleases. From eternity He knew, and that without any decree or foreordination, just precisely what the spirit and conduct of all of Christ's accusers would be, and consequently He framed the given or present plan right into the exigency of the times. This may also afford us a clue to the reason why Christ's advent and sufferings and death did not come earlier in the world's history, say right after the Fall. In that event there would not have been need of the long preliminary training of the world for His coming. The clue lies in this, viz., perhaps there never was a time in all the previous ages when all the factors requisite to Christ's vicarious death were present. Surely not one single feature of these dare be omitted from that ordeal, for otherwise Christ's death will not suffice. Now there are a large number of details involved, and it is very easy to see that some of these may never before this have been present; and therefore never before this time could the ordained plan be executed.

In this view of things, God is absolutely cleared from any complicity with sin, but He simply caused the self-induced wrath of men to praise Him.

In this view we also see that Redemption is a certain fact; for if all the factors of the present plan had never been developed (and we see that they might not have been), than another scheme was at hand, and another and another, so that we are sure of some scheme, without involving God in decreeing, or in any way conniving at, sin.

I now proceed to speak of the Person by whom Redemption is made and offered.

THE SON OF GOD.

There are several reasons why the Son of Man must also be the Son of God, in the one Person, Jesus Christ.

1. *To reveal God's love to man, and His earnest desire to save him.*

As a moral result of the Fall and the consequent derangement of man's soul-constitution, the creature does not only himself hate the Creator, but he is very positive that the Creator hates him. To eradicate this notion and to show that the opposite is really the case, there is no way more forceful and effectual than the gift of His dear Son, to live and work, to suffer and die, as He did, and of which I shall speak in another lecture. "Not sparing His own Son, but giving Him a ransom for us all," will make such an appeal to man that it will open the way for the indwelling of that Son to give established "life," and instead of "death," and to bring love and peace and joy, for hate and shame and sorrow.

2. *To subserve the end of redemption, loyalty to God.*

If God had caused a man to be born out of the order of nature, and so possibly sinless as Adam, or if he had caused an angel to become incarnate; if either of these had rescued man from sin, the one working such rescue would certainly challenge and receive the gratitude, praise and eternal worship of the rescued. Indeed, it could not be otherwise, for

7

the substitution rendered by one for another, especially when such substitution involves great hard-
ships, must be an irresistible appeal to the best and
noblest principles of the heart of the person helped.
Now this fact would plainly defeat the greatest end
in view in redemption, viz., as was stated before,
loyalty toward God, the Creator and Lord of all.
It would induce man to worship a creature rather
than the Creator. This would be an insult to
Heaven and a drawback to earth, inasmuch as man
cannot be under such circumstances what he must
be if his mind, heart and body go out toward God.
*Now the Son of God is God, and hence he who wor-
ships the Son worships the Father also; and thereby
is the purpose of God fulfilled.*

3. *Another reason why the Son of Man must also
be the Son of God is this, that the fullest and last
revelation of God and things may be made to the
world, and that the creative plan may be completed.*

There is first a realm of pure spirits. Afterwards, in the creation, there appeared the pure
material. In man the spiritual and material find
a point of unity. But there is a wide gulf between
this condition of the universe and God, the Infinite Spirit. Can this gulf be bridged? Yes, in
the Person of the God-man. In Him there is the

highest unity, the rounding out and completion of
the universe, for it inseparably connects the
universe with God. In this we behold the mind
of God in respect to His relation to the universe
which He created; therefore we find here not only
a completing of creation but also a revelation of
God, the Creator. Not a few most profound schol-
ars hold that the Son of God would have become
incarnate, in order to consummate what has been
here outlined, even if Adam had never sinned.

But as sin has entered the world, how much the
more is it necessary that God should reveal His
relation to the world and His will concerning it.
From this we perceive that it is a matter of the
utmost importance that this revelation should
come with most absolute authority; that He
should not speak through man of like infirmities
with us, but that he should speak directly, face to
face, Himself. *Now the Son of God is God, and
hence he who hears the Son hears the Father also.*

What evidences do we have that the Son of
Man was also the Son of God?

1. Predictions; 2. Christ's own declaration; 3.
Miracles; 4. The Father's testimony; 5. The tes-
timony of the Apostles; 6. Divine works; 7.
Divine attributes and Divine worship.

1. Predictions.

a. Isaiah, chapter vii. 14: "He shall be called Immanuel. For unto us a child is born, unto us a son is given, and the government shall be upon his shoulder; and His name shall be called Wonderful, Counsellor, The Mighty God, The Everlasting Father, The Prince of Peace."—ix. 6.

b. Jeremiah : "He shall be called the Lord our Righteousness."—xxiii. 6.

c. Micah : "But thou Bethlehem |Ephrata, though thou be little among the thousands of Judah, yet out of thee shall come forth one that is to be Ruler in Israel ; whose goings forth have been from of old from everlasting."—v. 2.

d. John the Baptist: "He it is who coming after me is preferred before me, whose shoe's latchet I am not worthy to unloose."—i. 27.

2. Christ's own declaration.

a. Matthew : "All power is given unto me in Heaven and on earth."—xxviii. 18. "Where two or three are gathered in my name there am I in the midst of them."—xviii. 20. "Lo, I am with you alway, even unto the end of the world."—xxviii. 20. "The High Priest said unto Him, I adjure thee by the living God that thou tell us whether thou be the Christ, the Son of God. Jesus said unto him, Thou hast said."—xxvi. 63.

b. John: "Before Abraham was I am."—viii.
58. "The Father hath committed all judgment
unto the Son, that all men should honor the Son
even as they honor the Father."—v. 22. "And
now, O Father, glorify thou me with thine own
self, with the glory which I had with thee before
the world was."—xvii. 5.

Many others of the same import.

3. Miracles. These are so numerous and so distinctive of Christ that nothing more than a mere
allusion need be made in this connection.

4. The Father's testimony.

a. At the Saviour's Baptism. "And, lo, the
heavens were opened, and he saw the Spirit of
God descending like a dove and lighting upon
Him. And, lo, a voice from heaven, saying, This
is my beloved Son, in whom I am well pleased."
Matthew iii. 16, 17.

b. On the Mount of Transfiguration. "This is
my beloved Son, in whom I am well pleased; hear
ye him." Matt. xvii. 5.

5. The testimony of the Apostles.

a. John: "In the beginning was the Word, and
the Word was with God, and the Word was God."
—i. 1. "This is the true God and eternal life."
1 John v. 20.

b. Thomas: "My Lord and my God."

c. Paul: In Christ "dwells all the fullness of the Godhead bodily." Col. ii. 9. "God was in Christ, reconciling the world unto himself." 2 Cor. v. 19.

6. Divine works.

a. John : "All things were made by Him and without Him was not any thing made that was made."—i. 3.

b. Paul: "By Him were all things created that are in heaven and on earth, visible and invisible." Col. i. 3, 4.

7. Divine Worship.

a. John: "That all men should honor the Son as they honor the Father. He that honoreth not the Son, honoreth not the Father who hath sent him." John v. 23, also Rev. v. 9–14.

b. Paul: "That at the name of Jesus every knee should bow, of things in heaven and things in earth and things under the earth, and that every tongue should confess that Jesus Christ is Lord, to the glory of God the Father." Phil. ii. 10 and 11. "Let all the angels of God worship him." Hebrews i. 6.

THE SON OF MAN.

I have pointed out several reasons why the Son of Man must also be the Son of God. I now advance to consider several reasons why the Son of God must also be the Son of Man.

1. *To subject Himself to the broken law.*

Any being, undertaking to deliver man from the curse of the law, must himself live under the law, to fulfil it in every jot and tittle. This it is that will give merit and value to his vicarious suffering and death. Now God as God, the Giver of the law, cannot possibly subject Himself to the law; for the law adapted to creatures, cannot be fulfilled by the Creator, unless He assumes human nature. Hence the Scriptures declare that "God sent his Son, made of a woman, made under the law, to redeem them that were under the law." "The Word became flesh, and dwelt among us." "Great is the mystery of godliness, God was manifested in the flesh." "But made himself of no reputation, and took upon him the form of a servant, and was made in the likeness of men."

2. *The Son of God must also be the Son of man for the purpose of attesting the scheme of salvation to man's mind and heart.*

In another section I have shown that the Divinity of Christ is necessary in order that when, by suffering and death, he rescues man, man will turn in piety and loyalty to the Creator and Lord, and not to a mere creature. But here I observe that the humanity of Christ is essential in order to subject him to suffering and death by which to purchase and attract man's loyalty and worship. Moreover, it is requisite that such an atonement should not be made save in the eye of man. Otherwise man will scarcely be induced to believe in its reality, and if he did, it would not, in the very nature of things, have the best effect on his character and life.

From the foregoing we reach the conclusion that the hypostatic union of the Son of God with the Son of Man was a logical and moral necessity.

The peculiar evidences of Christ's humanity are such as these: He was born, he grew in stature and in wisdom, He ate, He drank, He slept, He rested, He wept, He suffered and He died.

THE GOD-MAN.

From what we have seen under sections before, taken in connection with the testimony of the Scriptures which has been and might be quoted, it is very manifest that the Son of God and the Son of Man must be inseparably united in one person, the God-man.

There have been but a few men in the past history of the church who denied this truth and held to the notion that the two natures in Christ are independent and separable from eath other. But this opinion was so radically and openly unreasonable and unscriptural that it never gained any considerable foothold and recognition among Christians.

In respect to the hypostatic union of the two natures in the God-man, it is important to state a few points touching these natures as such. First, let us bear in mind that neither of these natures were persons at the moment of the conception and birth of Christ. The human nature never had a separate personal existence before the Incarnation. After the Incarnation it is true that the Saviour's human nature was such in all respects, possessing the very highest glory, inasmuch as it was the same as that of Adam before the Fall. But being from its very conception in conjunction with the divine nature, although retaining its own peculiarities, properties, and attributes throughout, the human never was anything more than one nature in the one Person. An analogy of this mystery is found in man. Man has two natures, spiritual and animal. Animal nature is found in independent and separate existence in, say, a horse. Spiritual nature is found in an angel. But in man the two natures are so completely united that they constitute but one person. In this union neither of these two natures has had an existence apart and before their union.

This analogy is mentioned to express only the mode of union between the two natures in the God-man, and not anything in regard to the existance or non-existence of the divine nature prior to this union.

When we turn to the oracles of God, we are at once taught that the divine nature in the God-man is none other than the Son of God, as considered before.

This leads to the logical conclusion that the Son of God assumed the Son of Man, that the former united Himself with the latter, the two together constituting the God-man. This is the Incarnation. "Great is the mystery of godliness; God manifest in the flesh."

We see by this that Christ's divine nature was truly a Person before the Incarnation. Accordingly at the moment of his conception by the Holy Ghost in the womb of the Virgin Mary, He who "thought

it not robbery to be equal with God, emptied himself and took upon him the form of a man." Here
we are taught that the Son of God veiled or put
aside the distinctive properties that constituted his
divine personality, in order to limit himself to a
divine nature only, which nature, with the human
nature united, constituted the one Person, the
God-man. If the question be asked, in what points
or parts did He limit Himself from personality to
nature?—I may answer, in all the physical attributes that belong to a divine Person, such as omniscience, omnipotence and omnipresence, as also
divine consciousness.

The history of the Saviour's childhood, boyhood
and manhood, compared with each other, teaches
us that the united natures in him, or the Person
of Christ, was unique and peculiar to the God-
man. In his childhood and youth the human
nature seems to have the ascendency—the divine
being entirely hidden. At the age of twelve the
divine nature advances, perhaps suddenly, so that
it is already clearly manifested. There may be
from this on a gradual development of the divine
up to the time of his baptism and the voice from
Heaven, saying: "This is my beloved Son in
whom I am well pleased." Certainly from this

time forth the God-man, owing not to His human, but to His Divine, nature, had developed into and possessed all the fullness of the God-head bodily; at the same time, owing not to His divine, but to His human, nature, He had developed into and possessed all the fullness of manhood bodily. That is to say, the God-man enjoyed all the perfections of Deity and humanity, bound together by one personal consciousness.

What can be said in respect to the relation and communication subsisting between the two natures of the God-man? In the case of man, the spiritual and animal natures each has its own peculiar sphere of activity. The spiritual cannot perform the work of the animal, nor can the animal that of the spiritual. However, by virtue of the fact that the spiritual nature is almost infinitely above the animal in man, it was shown that the animal functions are magnified by the spiritual nature. I refer to man in his pristine glory.

This I think analogous to what is found in Christ. Both natures have their own distinctive sphere of activity. But the divine in Christ, being infinitely above the human, has through contact and communication a magnifying and uplifting influence upon the human nature.

As in the activities of the two natures in man, that of each is ascribed and credited to the person —man: so also is the same done in the case of the Saviour. To illustrate: In man, the animal nature hungers, thirsts, sleeps, but we do not say that the animal *nature* does so, but we say the *man* hungers, thirsts, etc. So the spiritual nature reasons, worships, etc., but we do not ascribe this to the spiritual *nature*, but to the *man*. Now in the case of Christ, His divine nature is omniscient, omnipotent, etc., and His human nature labors, suffers, and dies. Yet all those attributes, functions and facts are not ascribed and credited to the respective *natures* to which they belong, *but to Jesus Christ, the God-man.*

In the light of the foregoing statements we may well believe the Apostle's words that "Christ is all in all"—in Creation, Redemption, Worship, and in Heaven. The God-man is the foundation and cornerstone of all true theology, as "He is the chief among ten thousand and the one altogether lovely," to every ransomed and sanctified soul. "To him, every knee must bow, of things in Heaven and of things on the earth and of things under the earth, and every tongue confess that Jesus Christ is Lord, to the glory of God the Father." The God-man

is the Way, the Truth, and the Life. He that
cometh to the Father must come through Him.

    " Ere the blue heavens were stretched abroad,
        From everlastiug was the Word;
    With God He was; the Word was God,
        And must divinely be adored.

    " By His own power were all things made,
        By Him supported all things stand :
    He is the whole creation's Head,
        And angels fly at His command.

    "But lo! He leaves those heavenly forms,
        The Word descends and dwells in clay,
    That He may converse hold with worms,
        Drest in such feeble flesh as they.

    "Mortals with joy behold His face,
        The eternal Father's only Son ;
    How full of truth! how full of grace!
        When through His form the Godhead shone.

    'Archangels leave their high abode,
        To learn new mysteries here, and tell
    The love of our descending God,
        The glories of Immanuel."

LECTURE V.

THE GOD-MAN'S MEDIATORIAL WORK,

1 TIM. ii. 5, 6.

1 Tim. ii. *5, 6.* For there is one God and one Mediator between God and man, the Man Christ Jesus; who gave himself a ransom for all, to be testified in due time.

LECTURE V.

THE last lecture was devoted to the discussion of the Person of the God-man. Three things were therein established, viz., that our Saviour has a divine nature, and a human nature, and that these two unite in one Person.

I now advance a step, to speak of the work which the God-man performed for our redemption, which is called the Mediatorial Work.

Let us here observe several facts. First, the fall had so affected man's intellect that it was obtuse and darkened. He could not any more clearly understand and compass God's law and precepts. He was also inflated with pride and self-will, so that he cared not to know. Accordingly we find that the teachers of God's Word, especially at the time of Christ's advent, gave themselves up to commenting on the silly comments of their predecessors, and not to the ascertainment of the mind of the Spirit in the Word. Second, the transgression of Adam and Eve had brought upon the whole human race the penalty of the law, which was

death—spiritual and eternal. Spiritual death came
at once; eternal death was a foregone conclusion,
inasmuch as that is nothing but spiritual death
extended beyond the confines of time. Now, to
overcome the former and avert the latter, satisfaction had to be made to God's moral attributes.

Third, the Fall had thrown man out of relation
and harmony with his Creator and Ruler. He
must be restored to an estate in which he can
again avail himself of such rites and ceremonies
and means of grace as God sees fit to give him for
the perfecting of his spiritual life.

These three points give us a clue to the offices
which Christ must assume as man's Redeemer,
namely, Prophet, Priest, and King.

PROPHET.

From the prophetic office Christ is called a
prophet in Deut. xviii. 18; Matt. xxi. 11; John vi.
14; Luke vii. 16, and xxiv. 19. An Evangelist in
Isaiah xli. 27. A Master in Isaiah l. 4, and lxiii. 1.
A Rabbi in Matt. xxiii. 8, 10; John. iii. 2.

As a Prophet it was incumbent on the Saviour
to give instruction in four particulars: the law and
the prophets, the past and the future. It was intimated a short time ago that the religious teachers

of the Jews were short-sighted and corrupt. They had so thoroughly glossed and blurred the Old Testament Scriptures that neither they nor the lay people understood their real meaning and import. This fact is only fully seen when we study the Sacred Books of those times—the Talmud, etc. However, Christ Himself brings forward some of their odious and defiled stuff in the Sermon on the Mount.

In general, it may be said that touching the Law, the Rabbis taught, and the people believed, they were blameless. The law was deprived of its inner spirit and demands, and, therefore, nothing but the letter remained, which they flattered themselves they had fulfilled by their rites and ceremonies, their long prayers and many alms-deeds. We can easily perceive how this took away all need of a spiritual Saviour. Thus Paul said, referring to his life in sin: "I was alive without the Law once, but when the Law came sin revived, and I died." Indeed the whole nation trusted in themselves that they were righteous, and that the rest of the world lay in sin and under the curse of God.

The God-man came forward therefore as a Prophet, and uncovered the moral law and divine precepts as promulgated in the Old Testament, particularly through Moses and the prophets, and declared that the law was spiritual and that they were carnal; that it demanded not only external decorum, but internal purity; that both Jews and Gentiles were alike under the law and that all alike were sinners, that none had nor could, unaided, meet its demands; that the law was an outward exponent of the character of God and His hatred to sin, and that while God required its fulfillment, no one could do so under a dispensation of works, but only in a dispensation of grace; that while it was truly a Rule of Life to the saint, it was a mere schoolmaster to the sinner to draw him to Christ, Himself, through whom needed grace was offered. He showed, furthermore, that the moral law and the divine precepts were not alone in revealing that "none is righteous, no, not one" and that "all have sinned and come short of the glory of God;" but that these were complemented and supported by the Levitical law. That this law was scarcely anything more than a tangible and concrete, instead of abstract, expression of the same imperative truths. That, accordingly, this law could not possibly take the place of a Redeemer from heaven, for it could not make the corner thereunto perfect. He insisted that both these sets of laws through Moses, and all the additional teachings of the prophets, were intended to exhibit right character and conduct, and not to create them. To obtain these they must "all be born again" by water and the Spirit. But this takes place alone by acceptance of Him who stood in the midst of them.

In respect of the predictions of the prophets concerning Christ and the glory of His kingdom, as might be expected, the rabbis were as far out of the way as in the case of the law. Believing themselves pure and unspotted as touching the law, it is patent that they would misinterpret the character and mission of the Messiah. Of course they would look for the advent of one who should bring deliverance. On account of disobedience, the Jewish government had fallen into the hands of the Romans. This Roman yoke was galling their necks, and was exceedingly odious to their dignity. Should they, the elect people of Jehovah, be subject to these Roman dogs? No ; this cannot, this dare not so remain. The Messiah spoken of by the old prophets must hasten his approach. We desire, we demand deliverance. Such language might have been uttered. Now, not recognizing their spiritual, but groaning under their civil, bond-

age, no wonder that they read and interpreted
their wishes and desires into those long-standing
prophecies. It is imperative, therefore, that this
"teacher come from God," should unearth and set
forth the true intent and meaning of all. We see,
accordingly, that on every proper occasion he se-
lects from the prophet's roll such passages as spoke
of the Messiah and His mission and work, and
then applies those sayings to Himself, at the same
time insisting on it that He is come for the purpose of establishing a spiritual kingdom and of de-
livering men from the bondage of death and the
power of the devil.

Again, in the matter of Christ's teaching concerning the present and the future, the following
may be profitably mentioned. In the nature of
things, the Old Testament dispensation was a training school. The people's minds were darkened to
such an extent that they could not take in the large
thoughts of God. As the people became prepared,
God meant to reveal more and more of His mind
and will. In point of fact this was done. The
coming of the God-man, however, marked an epoch
in the unfolding of the Father's purposes and will
in reference to the world, which also involves a
fuller revelation of man's relations and duties toward

both God and His fellow men. Many things remained to be said that were a *de novo* revelation.
Thus we find positive precepts, and underlying
principles in all His private and public teachings.
This is notably so in His mountain sermon.   So
also an advance step was taken in reference to the
disclosure of the future. This Prophet lifted the
vail from the future in many ways.   He spoke of
His own death, even in detail.   He spoke of the
sufferings and death of His apostles.   He prophe-
sied the persecutions that should come to His own
church.   He declared His kingdom's final success
and triumph. *He lifted the gates of Heaven, and
drew back the curtains of hell.*

Now bear in mind that in all these things Christ
spoke as one having authority.   No wonder that
the people were astonished.   Their stupid teachers
had caused them all to fall asleep, but here is a
Rabbi who enlightens their mind, thrills their
heart, and moves their will.   Nicodemus voices
their sentiment in saying: "We know that Thou
art a teacher come from God."

It is also profitable to observe in this place that
the Saviour's divine words were supported by His
divine works.   Just how far the people generally
were really benefited, spiritually, by His miracu-

lous works, it is impossible to tell. At the same time it is, doubtless, true that the ability to perform superhuman works was associated with, and, therefore, expected of Him who made claim of the Messiahship. While some may have been more prejudiced against Christ on *account* of His miraculous powers, it was certainly not owing to *lack of intellectual persuasion of the soundness of His claim, but rather to the perverseness and stubbornness of their hearts and wills, in spite of better knowledge.* Theirs was a clear case of sinning against light; and, in case of many, of blasphemy against the Holy Ghost. On the other hand, we have reason to believe that many of the common people accepted Him as their Redeemer and Lord, from the fact that He had healed their sick, opened the eyes of the blind, made the lame to walk, loosed the tongue of the dumb, and raised the dead.

In view of all this, Jesus may well challenge the people to believe His words for His very work's sake.

From all this we learn that Christ's office of Prophet was vitally essential to His mission as man's redeemer. He brought light into a dark place, and caused the world to see the day of her visitation. He showed knowledge in three all-important truths: man's depravity and helplessness, salvation and deliverance through a crucified and risen Saviour, and a day of "Judgment," followed by heaven and hell.

PRIEST.

The second office of the God-man is the priestly, or sacerdotal. In this capacity He redeems man, and reconciles God to man. In this office He performs the part of the Old Testament priest, who propitiated God by the sacrifice he offered for the people—which priest and sacrifice were a type of the true Priest, Jesus Christ. Unlike the Old Testament priest, Christ became both the offerer and the sacrifice, and therefore there was intrinsic and essential merit in it.

Theologians usually divide the sacerdotal office into two parts, one of which is designated as the Atonement, and the other as Intercession. The first of these was accomplished in full by Christ's earthly work ; the second is being carried on since His session at the right hand of God.

Atonement.—We do well at this juncture to stop and call to mind what I stated in the second lecture, "The Fall." It is this, in substance: The effect of the fall is two-fold, subjective and object-

ive. The subjective result is the disturbance of
man's spiritual constitution, etc. The objective
consequence has to do with the mind of God. God,
as Lawgiver, had promulgated a just and righteous
law, the sanctions of which were an adequate expression of His own character and relation to Adam
and Eve; as well as a rule of life and voice of warn-
ing to them. It promised "life" on one hand and
"death" on the other. In the transgression of this
law, "death" followed—this was subjective. But
this disobedience was also a crime. God was displeased with man. In a sense He had turned away
from man. His justice and holiness had been offended. He is a God of truth, and He had said in
the event of transgression they (Adam and Eve)
should surely die. However, "God is love," and
willeth not that any should die—eternally. Now
what can be done that He may be just and yet justify all who call upon His name? Here it is that
God lays hold on one who is "mighty to save and
strong to deliver." Please bear in mind that the
great end of redemption is the moral and spiritual
restoration of man. But in order to realize this
end, God must help man. In order, however, that
He may be justified in this, His justice and holiness and veracity must all be satisfied and vindi-

cated.   This can only be done through a substitute for man.

The first thing that substitute has to observe is the broken law of God.   This law must be kept inviolate, according to the original demand.   By this, two things are accomplished: God's holiness is established, and the substitute establishes His own merit and worthiness, and thereby brings Himself into a proper position for vicarious suffering for man.

Man himself could not possibly keep the law, for he is condemned by the law on account of original and actual sin.   The God-man, therefore, is born without sin, and although tempted and tried like as man is, He yet remains without actual transgressions.   He challenges even His bitter enemies to say aught against Him, but there is no accusation.

This is called Christ's active obedience, and is the imperative prerequisite to all His other work as priest.

As the God-man becomes man's substitute in fulfilling the demand of the law, so also does He take man's place in suffering the penalty of the violated law.   Let us see how this is.   Some maintain that Christ suffered the exact equivalent that man would suffer eternally, if he were not ransomed and restored. Rendering the exact equivalent, God was plainly justified to remit the penalty on man and turn favorably to him. This I do not believe, for two reasons: First, It is utterly impossible for Jesus Christ to suffer an exact equivalent of man's suffering in time and eternity. For the principal factors in man's suffering is consciousness of sin and pain of conscience. Now neither of these factors can possibly be transferred to Christ. As a substitute, I readily conceive how the sins of men lay heavily on His heart, and weighed mightily on His body. In view of His unique person as God-man His sufferings could have infinite merit; but still all this is not identical and equivalent suffering.

Second, if the above proposition were literally true then, in justice to man, the subjective result of his transgression ought to be fully and completely abrogated, and he ought to be brought back to his original estate. This is not mere sentiment, but the demand of strict justice. If the God-man literally suffers the literal penalty resting on man —I use the word man as standing for humanity— then God has certainly no more fault to find with man, and we are all of us pure as the angels.

Of two things, however, I am fully persuaded, viz., that God will not deal unjustly with man, and that man manifestly is still suffering the penalty of the law as he is naturally engendered.

What, accordingly, can the work of atonement mean? If Christ did not literally suffer the penalty of the broken law, what did He do and suffer? I answer, He suffered sufficiently in body and mind during a number of years' sojourn on the earth, and particularly in the garden and on the cross, to balance and satisfy the objective result of the Fall— the offended mind of God.   Now it is not for man, the offender, to say how much the God-man is compelled to suffer to make an atonement.   That belongs to God, the offended.   This much only may be ventured, and that is, that His sufferings must be adequate to show man that God is just, and true to His word; but also that He is infinite in love, in that He spared not His own Son, but laid on Him the iniquity of us all; and that by His stripes we are healed.   In view of Christ's Person, His suffering, of whatever character it may be, and however long or short a period it may extend, has infinite merit, and so God may well be justified to set it down to our credit.   By the God-man's passive obedience, all the obstacles and hindrances are re-

moved, and God is enabled to come to the rescue
of man, to deliver him from the subjective consequences of the Fall. Hereby does this Priest offer
himself as a sacrifice to God for the purpose of
propitiating and reconciling Him to man. In this
view of the atonement, I clearly see how all men
everywhere must of necessity still be dead by nature, and, therefore, suffering the broken law in its
subjective effect, both in time and in eternity, while
at the same time the objective effect is covered and
canceled. Our High Priest purchased the favor of
God, by which it is possible for all men to be saved,
but this sacrifice did not absolutely restore man.
Personal salvation comes only to such as accept the
sacrifice of Christ by faith. This subject will be
called up again at another place.

Intercession.—The Atonement made by His active and passive obedience is not the only work of
Christ. As Priest, seated at the right hand of the
Father, the Scriptures teach that He is active in
interceding for them whom He purchased with His
blood. He pleads His own merits in man's behalf.
Whether this part of Christ's sacerdotal office is
absolutely necessary for man's salvation, I know
not. Judging from a purely philosophical standpoint, I would infer that it was not. However,

this is certain, that hereby the Redeemer shows His intense interest in poor fallen humanity. He will not be passive, as He might be justified to be, but earnestly active, in general for all men, and especially for the regenerate, through all time. Let us catch the spirit and zeal of our High Priest, and intercede devotedly and earnestly for all our brethren, at the throne of prayer and grace, and so become the means of turning many to righteousness.

KING.

In the God-man's third office, we have His exercise of the regal function. In the interest of a better understanding of this office, the reign of Christ is usually divided into three parts, called the reign of Power, of Grace, and of Glory.

The Kingdom of Power.—Creation is ascribed to the Son of God, the Second Person in the Holy Trinity. The Apostle John says, "All things were made by Him, and without Him was not anything made that is made." In virtue of this fact Christ is, properly, ruler over all things that He created, and His reign extends over all things visible and invisible, living and dead. As long as we hold fast to a personal, living Christ, it matters not so much whether we know the exact *modus operandi*

of the creation; for we are thoroughly assured that
nothing could have come into existence without
Him, and that nothing could abide but by His
almighty hand.   I can express in one sentence my
creed in reference to the method of creation.   It is
this: I believe, in the light of the Bible and of
science, that some existing things, as they now are,
have come through a gradual development or evolution, and that the major part have come immediately and directly by the fiat of God. "He spake,
and it was done."

In respect of the regal authority and activity of
the King, I aver with the utmost emphasis that He
has immediate supervision and direct control over
all that exists, and that if He should remove His
presence for a moment from any part of the Universe, all would come to grief and desolation.   I
believe that the laws in nature are naught but the
modes of the Deity's orderly reign, and that the
forces in nature can all be resolved into one force,
the will of God.

The kingdom of power also implies Christ's
dominion over animals, men and devils.   While
all these have a certain delegated realm and free-
dom for the activity of.their respective natures,
still there is a Supreme Ruler over them who will

never abdicate His throne. Christ's reign of power directs the stars in their courses, and causes the wrath of men and devils to praise Him.

The Kingdom of Grace.—At another place in this lecture I said: "The Fall has thrown man out of relation and harmony with his Creator and Ruler. He must be restored to an estate in which he can make use of such rites, ceremonies and means of grace as God sees fit to give him for the perfecting of his spiritual life." This "estate" is Christ's kingdom of grace, the church. Justified by faith, the believer is transplanted from the "world" to the church, in which the very means he needs are deposited and dispensed. In this kingdom, "law" and "force" are transmuted into love, which is both "law" and "force" of another kind and of a more excellent character. I will not anticipate here what must be left for another place, but merely to say that not a part or particle is lacking in this kingdom, that it is philosophically apparent ought to be present. Provision is here made for man's separation from deadly influences; for the nourishment and development of spiritual life; for the dispensation of grace to the whole world; and for the training of all the saints for the kingdom of glory.

9

The Kingdom of Glory.—Of this a certain writer says: "Christ most gloriously rules the chuch triumphant in heaven, and fills it with eternal felicity, to the praise of the divine name and the refreshment of the saved, to which belong all the inhabitants of heaven, the good angels and redeemed men. They behold the Lord in His glory, as He shows Himself to the dead when He awakens them to life. This glory of the Lord begins with the time of His ascension to heaven, but will not be perfectly unfolded until, after the final judgment, believers also will enter into the kingdom of His glory to share with Him its possession. In this kingdom the righteous shall see the King in His beauty, for He is the chief among ten thousand, and the one altogether lovely." *Hail, blessed kingdom; all hail, thrice blessed King! Prophet, Priest and King. In these three offices there is one Mediator between God and man, the God-man, Christ Jesus.*

LECTURE VI.

THE CHURCH.

MATT. xvi. 18.

Matt. xvi. *18.* Upon this rock will I build my church ; and the gates of hell shall not prevail against it.

LECTURE VI.

At this point two ways are open before us. The subject of man's spiritual recovery might here be taken up, following logically the subject of the preceding lecture ; or we may give attention to the means and instrumentalities through which his recovery is effected. The latter I think to be better suited to my purpose, and I enter, therefore, upon that way first.

The agency that first claims our attention, is the Church. This institution is variously designated in the Old and New Testaments as the Church, the Kingdom of Heaven, the Kingdom of God, the Church of God, and the Church of Christ. Properly considered, the Church of God had its beginning with the inhabitants of Eden. There were two persons only, it is true; and in a real sense these two constituted a family, united as they were for the purpose of introducing the human species, and for domestic life and enjoyment. However, inasmuch as their spiritual life and noblest felicity depended on union with their

Creator, which union was to be perpetuated through obedience to law and the observance and use of means and agencies adapted to their needs; and inasmuch as this man and woman were set at first to worship their Lord and King, and to keep His name uppermost in the minds of their descendants, there are here found the true marks of God's kingdom on earth, and the best realization of its divine ideal.

In view of God's purpose to redeem the world by his Son the Church was not destroyed even after the Fall. Through all the ages before the advent of Christ, she remained among men.

In the reconstruction epoch, when the God-man redeemed the world, the ancient Church received some changes. In the Old Testament dispensation, when the people were in training for the Messiah, it was needful that there should be certain rites and ceremonies adapted solely for that period, and therefore temporary. But when the last dispensation is ushered in, it becomes necessary that the imperfect give way to the perfect, and the temporary to the permanent. The Church of Christ, accordingly, is properly characterized as perfect, on her divine side.

This last sentence brings me to a thought which

is somewhat in the nature of a definition of the Church. To my view the Church consists of two parts, *the divine-spiritual*, and the human-material. In the divine part we find Christ, the founder and corner-stone, and the means of grace, and all the ceremonies and ordinances, on their spiritual side. In the human-material part there are all those who stand connected with her, together with the physical elements constituting the means of grace, and all purely human inventions, which may be good and useful and expedient, but nothing more.

From this standpoint it is easy to see the possibility of the Church becoming corrupt, and Luther was right when he spoke of the Church being in Babylonish captivity during a thousand years previous to his time. At the same time, it is most important to note that in another and higher sense the Church is never anything but pure and unspotted. When one speaks of an imperfect or corrupt church, one must always remember that the human-material part is meant, and never the divine-spiritual. When we take account of the many human inventions that have been added at different periods in different branches of the Church's existence, and when we think of the

multitudes of precious souls that have thereby
been snared into hell, it is a great relief and joy,
and a matter of grateful praise to God, that Christ's
Church, as founded by Him, is very simple and un-
encumbered, and at the same time all comprehensive in her scope and influence.

In the preceding lecture, I remarked that the
scope or end of Christ's "Kingdom of Grace" is
the "training of all the saints for the Kingdom of
Glory."

That I hold to be true as a matter of course. To
realize this final purpose, hovever, "all the saints"
must be first fashioned out of "the wicked world."
It is necessary, accordingly, that the Church should
be a zealous propaganda. The wicked must be
overcome by the means of grace—the Word and
Sacraments. The devil must be cast out of them,
they must be clothed and put in their right minds,
and caused to sit at Jesus' feet. They must be incorporated with the Church, become a part of her
human side. This carving of saints out of such
unsightly material, or, in other words, this con-
quering of death and engrafting of life, is carried
on by Christ and man in hearty co-operation.
Thus the two parts of the Church are represented
in the conquest of the world. In this we find the

personal holding the impersonal—the means of grace—in hand, achieving the first object of the Church, to wit, to bestow life upon the dead, and to bring them within her sacred precincts, that by their free and constant use of her ordinances they may become "perfect and thoroughly furnished unto every good work." This implies that all who are thus added to the Church, do not only try to grow into the full stature of the Lord themselves, but also at once take their places as propagators of the Church. By this two-fold life—of taking in and giving out—there is "training of all the saints for the kingdom of glory."

The means of grace in the Church will receive further and separate treatment, each by itself, in succeeding lectures. It therefore remains that in this lecture the Church must be treated mainly on her strictly human side. Hence what will be said from this onward is meant to point out some of her attributes and characteristics.

ATTRIBUTES OF THE CHURCH.

It is the purpose of her Founder and Head that the Church cover the whole earth. Wherever sin abounds it is designed that grace shall much more abound. In view of this fact, one of the attributes of the Church is *Universality.*

The ancient Israelites believed that God's kingdom in their day was intended to include only
themselves. Indeed, generally speaking, there
was some truth in the belief. It is, hence, not to
be expected that great missionary enterprises
should be planned and executed. All this is
changed, however, in the Christian dispensation.
Jesus Christ manifested the true missionary spirit
on all proper occasions. If the Scribes, Pharisees
and others turn away from Him, He turns at once
to the Gentiles. During His earthly life He healed
so many "foreigners and aliens," both bodily and
spiritually, that doubtless it were surprising to
know the number. Christ's works of mercy were
also accompanied by His words of glad tidings.
He made bold to say, the offences thereby engendered notwithstanding, that the kingdom which
He came to establish was designed to embrace
all the nations of men. "Whosoever will may
come." But all His words and works on this side
of Calvary were transfigured into a brilliant
"Great Commission" on the other side, and just
before His ascension: "Go ye therefore, and teach
all nations, baptizing them in the name of the
Father and of the Son and of the Holy Ghost;
teaching them to observe all things whatsoever I

have commanded you, and, lo, I am with you alway, even unto the end of the world." Ten days after this, this commission is begun, in dead earnest, to be carried into execution. Three thousand souls were added to the Church—of all tongues, and climes, and nations of the earth. The Apostles go and teach all nations, one this way and another that, here and there and everywhere, suffering sore trials and persecutions for Christ's and the Kingdom's sake, but never fearing and never daunted. History records the fact that the early ages of Christianity were distinctively and decidedly missionary years; and it is very likely that by the end of the first century the Gospel was preached literally in every nation, and to every creature. The four or five succeeding centuries of controversy and settling of dogmas so largely superseded the missionary spirit that comparatively little was achieved. During this period the Church gained immensely in *intension*, but lost greatly in *extension*. The "dark ages" followed, and Satan regained the ground which he had lost in the days of Christ and the Apostles. From the time of the Reformation dates a fresh impulse to "lengthen the cords and strengthen the stakes of Zion." It remained, however, for the present century to catch fully the spirit of Christ, and to lift aloft a banner with this ensign: "*Christ for the world and the world for Christ.*" "*In hoc signo vinces,*" *is now the exulting shout of every true soldier of the Church's mighty host.*

It need scarcely be said that the attribute which we are now considering belongs to the Church by virtue of her essential nature. The very character of the Christian Church is such that she has a universal adaptation to the infinite number and variety of needs of the lost world. There is no depravity so deep, no sin so flagrant, no vice so offensive, nor sorrow so bitter, nor burden so oppressive, nor any other distress and calamity so great, for which the Church does not have a pardoning, life-giving, cleansing, uplifting and comforting virtue, power and influence. *Men may be polluted, crushed and groaning outside the Church, but inside, never. In her is the Great Physician, and a Balm of Gilead for every wound. In ages past millions have been touched and healed. To-day, four hundred millions live to call her blessed.*

Now, such essential adaptability does not exist in any other religion on earth. Mohammedanism was at the beginning propagated by the sword, and continues to flourish by reason of the vices which

it allows to its adherents. Confucianism, Buddh-
ism and all the other *isms* of the eastern empires
hold their place rather because they destroy and
obliterate the rational religious cravings and faculties of the soul than that they quicken and satisfy
them. This fact is acknowledged by the most
acute adherents of these religions, at the same time
that they attest to the infinite superiority of Christianity over their own.

Another attribute of the Church is *Visibility.*
The original conditions of admission were two—
repentance and faith. All, accordingly, who made
solemn profession of these two, were at once received. Naturally enough, it so happened that
there were many false professors; nevertheless if
their conduct was not grossly sinful and offensive
they still held their place. All, therefore, of every
description, who had been formally admitted to the
Church formed an external and visible society for
the public administering of the means of grace, and
the preaching of the gospel, and the mutual edification of each other. While the Church was one
unbroken whole, those living in any one city or
community united in a local society. At first all
the local churches may have been governed by
the same rules, and worshipped in the same forms.

Such outward and visible organization was essential, not only for the purpose above indicated, but also to the end of missionary operations. This for two reasons: First, in order to present a united and determined front to the unchristian people; and second, in order that they might have a common policy, or plan and principle of activity. Mere zeal without a definite plan of campaign would not conquer the world for the Master. Hence in the Acts we find that the Apostles repeatedly appealed to the decision of the elders and brethren at Jerusalem.

In the light of a remark I made in a previous paragraph, it is quite patent that although in external and visible relation to the Church, not all so related were truly Christian. There were many "tares" among the "wheat." This fact suffices to introduce a third attribute, namely, *Invisibility*. All who belong to the visible Church are called, but a few only of these are chosen: these constitute the invisible Church. Not every one who says Lord, Lord, will enter into the kingdom of glory, but he who doeth the will of the Father. As in the Jewish Church before Christ, so will it always be in the Christian Church, that many appear like whited sepulchres, but inwardly are vile

and full of corruption. There are many who have
a name to live, but are dead in trespasses and sin.
These have a name and place in the visible Church.
On the other hand, in all periods of the Church's
history there have been those who were in fact
just what they were in name. Christ's kingdom
is in them as well as around them. They believe,
and so obey the will of God. When the King in
His glory comes to make up His jewels, these are
the ones that will be chosen.

The Scripture texts that justify this attribute are
the following: Eph. v. 27, Mark ix. 38–40, Matt.
xv. 22, Matt. xiii. 24–30, Matt. vii. 21, John vi. 37,
xvii. 26.

Unity is a fourth characteristic of the Church.

By this is not meant that external connection of
churches which is adored and practiced by the
Romish church, and also praised by many Protestants, but a moral unity. A great and pious theo-
logian explains it thus: The import of this term is,
that all who worship God according to the doctrine
of Jesus Christ shall regard themselves as members
of one society, and as such should exercise mutual
brotherly love; that notwithstanding all differences
of birth, conditions, knowledge, opinion and forms,
they should still constitute one Church, or religious

society, worshipping one and the same Lord, even Christ, and partaking in common of the blessings promised to his followers. That there should be such a union was the last will and testament of Christ—John xiii. 34, xv. 1. In order to this, it is not essential that there should be a full and entire agreement of opinion on every particular doctrine. Christians, though differing as to their modes of thinking, their particular opinions and forms, and though divided into particular communions, ought to regard themselves as still but one Church, and so live together in unity of spirit. This is the true spirit of Christianity; it infuses feelings of toleration. The more one has of the mind of Christ, the more tolerant will he be to others, and especially because he knows that not only his Lord, but his brethren, see much in him which requires forbearance."

A fifth attribute is *Sanctity*.

Generally speaking the whole Church may be designated by this term, by reason of her superior and exalted station in the earth. Infinitely above every other society, when we take account of her divine-spiritual side, there is no difficulty to see the reason why she is sometimes called a holy Church, even when at the same time great corrup-

tion is manifest among her members. Thus the
Jews were called a holy people, at the same time
that they were shamefully wicked.

It is proper to say that the term "holy" in such
a connection does not predicate moral purity, but
merely emphasizes the fact that the institution in
which they stand is holy and divine. Specifically
stated, it is true that it is the very end of the
Church to create true holiness in the hearts of all
whom she embraces. While some resist this purpose and so will never belong but to the visible
Church, many do yield themselves to the Church's
grace, and are made clean and holy. In this connection the term "Sanctity" has reference to
moral character; and all those who are holy belong
not only to the visible but also to the invisible
Church.

The last attribute which I shall mention is *Per-
petuity*. In the very nature of the case the Church
must endure while the earth stands. The empire
of Satan must be matched, and finally overcome
by the empire of Christ. These two stand over
against each other; and since the former is likely
to hold a place till the consummation of all things,
so will also the latter; *the former decreasing and
the latter increasing*. This does not preclude the

10

fact that the human side of the Church will suffer
many changes from time to time.   Creeds, polity,
rites and ceremonies of to-day may possibly be
superseded by others to-morrow; not always because those of to-day are wrong and useless, but
rather because they have served their day, and
those of to-morrow are better for to-morrow.   In
plain and simple language, the meaning of the
foregoing is this: as the world is progressing in
thought and intelligent activity, it may be possible that old forms and methods of church-life will
give way to new ones, that are abreast of the times.
Note, also, that this reference is solely to things
human, and not to things divine.   It is plain,
therefore, that many of the old treasures of the
Church, which have been handed down from ancient times, are not now and never will be out-
grown and obsolete, because they have the mark
of divinity upon them.

It may also come to pass that where the Church
flourishes to-day she may decline hereafter.   This
is not to be ascribed to the will of God, but to the
perversity of men, as witness the once thriving
condition of the Eastern church and her feeble existence now.

Nevertheless, in spite of all the changes and vicissitudes through which the Church is forced to pass, she will abide while time lasts, for the "gates of hell shall not prevail against her." *When the end of the ages has come, having fulfilled her mission on the earth, the Church militant will be transfigured into the Church triumphant, to be the spotless and immortal bride of the King of kings and Lord of lords in heaven forever.*

THE MINISTRY.

Our conception of the Church would not be complete without a brief discussion of her ministry.

In the preceding lecture, the God-man, in his office as King, was said to have a Kingdom of Grace on earth in which He rules. That is true, and this makes Him the Supreme Head of the Church. It was He who first preached the gospel of the kingdom. His visible departure from among men called for others to take His place as teachers and preachers and earthly ambassadors. Accordingly, at the very beginning of Christ's redemptive career He gathered twelve men around Himself, to train and discipline and prepare them for service in His church. These were called Apostles. Two others were afterwards chosen, one to take the place of the traitor, and the other to fill a special mission among the Gentile nations.

It may be stated here that the Apostles of Christ exercised functions peculiar to themselves. They were to found churches in various parts of the world, and have the general superintendence over them. In order to prove the authenticity of their calling, Christ endowed them with the power of performing miracles, which they used when circumstances demanded it. Such supernatural works as Christ Himself performed, they were also empowered to do, to impress the world that their calling was not of man, but of God.

In point of fact, all the members of the Christian Church are kings and priests before the Lord, and all alike have the right to teach and rule. There is a sense in which it may be said that where a right or privilege belongs equally to all, such right or privilege can be exercised by none; for in the event of such exercise there would be endless confusion and disorder. Such would be the case in an absolute democracy in civil government, and such would likewise be the result in the Church. So far, there is no great dispute. At this point, however, two ways part. One party holds that a call to the ministry is traced back through the line of the ministry to the Apostles, and from them, of course, to Christ; that ordination is not a mere human expedient, but a laying on of consecrated hands, through which the Head of the Church confers authority and power. Another class holds and teaches that a right call emanates from the Church as such, and that it is not in any proper sense traced to Christ and the Apostles. The fact is, to be sure, recognized that the Church has no right to call any man to her altar without proper mental and moral qualifications, and that these qualifications are the gift of Christ. In the matter of ordination, it is held that "ordination of a teacher is nothing else than a public approval and confirmation of his calling to the office of teaching; so that thenceforward he may begin his work and enjoy his rights." Now, whatever others may hold respecting this very important subject, my own conviction is decidedly against the latter view.

What has been said touching the fact that all alike are kings and priests before the Lord, and all have a right to teach and preach, is true. The only question is whether those who have this natural right, which is one of the many blessings growing out of redemption, are commissioned to transfer their right to a certain number among them, which would constitute a right call, or whether the Head of the Church reserves the prerogative to do that for

the Church. I am fully persuaded that the latter
position is the correct one. The office of the ministry is entirely too important and responsible to
commit a call thereto to the Church immediately.
I do not believe that the Church has ever been in
an intellectual and moral position to qualify her to
judge who shall and who shall not be set apart to
this blessed calling. I believe that it would make
the highest calling on earth too dependent on
human caprice. My opinion is that it is attributa-
ble to this erroneous notion that the people generally, in our day, have comparatively small reverence for the ministry, and take little heed of what
they say and urge. Shall I say it? Yes, I will:
to this same false doctrine I ascribe the fact that
entirely too many ministers have waived and lost
the proper dignity which attaches to their position;
they make themselves entirely too cheap. This
evil is manifested in and out of the pulpit. I feel
doubly sure that if all ministers and people would
recognize the fact that the "Ambassador for Jesus"
is called, not of the Church but of Christ, there
would be unspeakable gain.

In this view of the call, Jesus Christ holds His
place as Head over all things in the Church.
Through the regular ministry which originated

with the Apostles, He calls whom he has before prepared by His grace in body, mind and spirit, inducts him into the office by the laying on of the hands of the presbytery, through which He imparts gifts and grace to qualify for the arduous and responsible duties resting upon him. Read Paul's charge to Timothy.

Called of God, the true minister holds himself responsible to God, and not in the least to men. In such a case all his words and works come with authority. He can say from his heart of hearts, "I AM hath sent me unto you," and when he speaks he can truly say, "Thus saith the Lord." Knowing in his very soul that he is directly authorized by the King to speak in His name, his gracious messages will have no uncertain sound, and his ruling and disciplining functions will not lack energy and stamina.

The last sentence I have to utter on this subject, which satisfies the scope of my address, can be framed as follows: *The ministry is taken out of the bosom of the Church, belongs most truly to the Church as part and constituent, is called by the Lord per se, is dedicated by a special gift of grace in ordination, is directly responsible to the Head of the Church for all conduct, and is thus literal am-*

bassador in a Kingdom, and not a mere office-bearer in a Republic; and hence, the terms "kings" and "priests," as applied to each member of the Christian Church, have their meaning exhausted by referring them to each Christian's individual and private relation to God and His Kingdom—this and nothing more.

LECTURE VII.

THE DIVINE REVELATION,

2 TIM. iii. 16.

2 Tim. iii. *16.* All Scripture is given by inspiration of God, and is profitable for doctrine, for reproof, for correction, and for instruction in righteousness.

LECTURE VII.

In my view the necessity of a divine revelation is self-evident.

By the five senses of our physical constitution we discover the phenomena of nature; by the Understanding we come to a knowledge of the sub-. stance which is beneath and behind phenomena; and by the Reason we discover somewhat of the principles, and forces, and laws beneath and behind substance.

Placing together all that we learn in these three ways, I think I am safe to say that the conclusion of every man, in a normal state of mind, is that there is an All-wise and All-powerful Being, who is called God. This it is that gives us a clue to the meaning of the Scripture which says: "For His invisible things, even His eternal power and God-head since the creation of the world, are clearly seen, being understood by the things that are made." I am very sure, however, that the light afforded by Nature and Reason has its limitations, when unassisted by Him who created both and set their bounds. .

The truth of the matter is, that all who are born under the light of a miraculous revelation, are really unable to speak with undoubted authority touching the definite character and amount of knowledge, science and philosophy can render us on purely divine and spiritual matters. The reason for this is, from infancy up through childhood and youth the light of the Bible inevitably falls upon the mind and brings superhuman knowledge. The very atmosphere of Christian countries is impregnated with the knowledge of God; and if it were the case, as it is in a few instances, that parents made an effort to isolate their children from all scriptural teaching, that they might have naught but the light of Reason to guide and influence them, it is absolutely impossible to effect their wish and will. Environed as we are, do what one will, Divine light will obtrude itself on the tablets of the mind.

This truth I give as showing that what philosophers deem as a purely mental result of the knowledge which they possess of supernal truths, is not so in fact; for imperceptibly and unconsciously to them they have all the time carried on their labor under the certain and positive teaching of the Word of God. Hence I emphasize the assertion that we dare not boast too much of the knowledge we have and can have of the mind and will of God apart from a divine disclosure of them.

Believing, as I do, that some knowledge of the character and will of God can be obtained by the discursive operations of the Understanding and the intuitions of Reason, without an immediate and divine revelation, the fact still remains that to the end of man's salvation, with all that is involved therein, he needs to know almost infinitely more than is embraced in the foregoing concession. Perhaps very few people have any conception of the character and extent of the things man ought to know in order to satisfy his ever-active mind and to perfect his life; and which is all, or nearly all, outside of the limitations of both "Pure" and "Practical" Reason (Kant). Following are the subjects which I think are included in this catalogue, to wit: God; the creation; origin of evil; redemption in Christ; means of grace, and the Holy Ghost; new obedience; immortality of the soul; heaven and hell. These topics, I think, cover, but not more, the demands of man's mental and spiritual nature and the eternal plan of God in reference to his being and destiny.

Now, the necessity of a God-made discovery of

these matters is perhaps best seen by examining
the knowledge preserved by men who were and are
minus such discovery, and hence who have nothing
but the much-vaunted light of Nature and Reason
to govern them.

In respect to God there were and are a multiplicity of discordant notions. Some writers, as
Max Müller and others, declare that there are
many evidences to indicate that the earliest or
oldest belief in God was monotheistic. Granted. .
This only goes to show that the original revelation
from God was passed down among succeeding generations of men, and while in many respects the
people had already become heathen—in worship
and practical life—they still clung to this traditional knowledge. Coming down through the
ages, and after all traditional, but supernatural,
knowledge was effaced and obliterated, the historic
fact stares us in the face that there were many who
even denied the existence of a God or gods, while
others believed in a multiplicity of gods, and still
others were either pantheists or deists. The historian Gibbon writes: "The philosophers diligently practiced the ceremonies of their fathers,
devoutly frequented the temples of their gods;
and sometimes, condescending to act a part on

the theatre of superstition, they concealed the
sentiments of an atheist under sacerdotal robes.''
As might be expected, out of such discordant
opinions grew the disgusting polytheism and idolatry practiced then and now in heathen nations.

The knowledge of one true and living God in
three persons, Father, Son and Holy Ghost, who
is perfect in all divine attributes, omniscient,
omnipresent, omnipotent, love, justice and mercy,
is more truly foreign to their minds than to the
new-born babe of Christian parents.

The *worship* of the heathen was and is not in
the least superior to their *knowledge*. Enlightened Athens, with all her great philosophers, was
full of statues and fanes, dedicated to their numerous gods. So, also, Rome. But even in these
cities the vilest and most diabolical worship was
conducted. ''Prostitution, with all its deformi-
ties, was systematically annexed to various pagan
temples, was often a source of revenue, and was,
in some countries, compulsory upon the female
population.'' Besides the number of men who
were killed in the bloody sports and spectacles, instituted in honor of the deities, human sacrifice was
offered to propitiate them. Boys were whipped on
the altar of Diana, sometimes until they died.

How many infants did the Carthaginians sacrifice
to their implacable god, Molech? What numbers
of human victims, in times of public danger, did
they immolate, to appease the resentment of the
offended deities? But travelers and missionaries
tell us that what was true anciently is true now—
there is not one particle of improvement. It is
but right to say that a few of the greatest and best
in all the different nations and ages of the past and
present disapproved of a great deal of the vice and
worship prevalent among them, but in spite of all
that, the people continued to "perish for lack of
knowledge."

As we pass on to a knowledge of creation, nothing worth the name was enjoyed. The peripatet-
ics held that the world was eternal; Democrites
taught that the present order of things came by a
fortuitous concourse of atoms; the Epicureans decided that it was made by chance, and others did
not account for it at all. Now, the significant
thing about all these opinions is, that they ruled
God entirely out of creation. If it be said, "Well,
these false conceptions are not a trifle worse, and,
indeed, not much different from those held by
some wiseacres of the present day," I have to
answer, No, that is true; but this does not make

the ancient philosophers any better, it only stamps those of our time as worse. The only difference between the two classes is that the ancients did not know better, because they had no divine revelation, and the moderns do not know better, because they discard such revelation. Like moles, they love to dig in the dark. In the final analysis, both classes are found to be heathen; one class of the head, and the other of the heart.

What has been said concerning creation is equally applicable to the origin of evil in the world. Ancient philosophers saw and lamented human depravity. In their speculations they always conceded that the race of man had fallen from a lofty position. They could not give satisfactory answers to when? how? why? Some of them fell on this theory, namely, "There are two original and eternal principles—God and matter. God is the author of all good; matter the author of all evil. Man's soul is spirit, and hence good; man's body is matter, and hence evil. Depravity was, accordingly, confined to the physical nature, and, therefore, the sooner the soul became disengaged from the body the better. From this originated the doctrine of the transmigration of the soul. Of course, no one feels to chide them for this fallacy. They had, be

11

it noted, the light of Nature and of Reason, and this is the result. With the same sources of knowledge the conclusion will never be more satisfactory, for neither science nor philosophy know, or can know, a whit about this subject.

This notion of the origin and character of depravity did not make any room for redemption. It is true that Plato, and perhaps a few others, seem to have some faint ray of light in this direction—just enough to make the surrounding darkness all the blacker. The light of nature afforded them some conception of the goodness of God, which a few among the wisest took as data upon which to base a hope of deliverance, in some way and at some time. But of the plan of atonement through which God may justify all and still continue just Himself, they knew absolutely nothing. Nature and Reason both teach: "The soul that sinneth shall die." Mercy, repentance, pardon, substitution, etc., are entirely foreign to the tenets of these teachers; and this is why the most cultivated philosophers could not and cannot now evolve a plan of salvation. Whatever hope they may have had was but a rope of sand. "Their house was left unto them desolate."

In the light of the foregoing remarks, it is need-

less to say that nothing was known of means of
grace, of the Holy Ghost, and of new obedience.
Relative to the immortality of the soul there was
great confusion of mind. The brightest lights
among the Greeks and Romans were Aristotle,
Socrates, Plato, Cicero and Seneca. Not one of
these speaks with a certain sound. It does not
seem unlikely that Aristotle denied immortality.
Socrates and Plato were undoubtedly very hopeful
of life hereafter. Just before his death the former
expressed himself as follows: "I hope I am now
going to good men, though this I would not take
upon me dogmatically to assert; but that I shall
go to the gods, who are absolutely good, I affirm.
For this reason I do not take it hard that I am to
die, as otherwise I should do; but I am hopeful
that there is something remaining for those who
are dead, and that it will then be much better for
good than for bad men." Still later he said to his
friends: "I am going out of the world and you
will remain in it; but which has the better, is a
secret to all but God." Plato, the noblest of the
disciples of Socrates, held similar opinions with
his teacher; while others of his disciples denied
immortality. Cicero was one of the strongest
advocates of the soul's immortality, and yet his

mind wavered more or less, like that of all the rest. After 'advancing a number of arguments to show "the reason of the faith that was in him," he declared—"which of these is true, God alone knows; and which the more probable, is a very grave question." Seneca asserts that immortality was rather promised than proved by their great men.

Again, and lastly, the heathen had no foundation in regard to heaven and hell. The language of Socrates, above quoted, is in point. Many of the wisest and the purest believed that these places existed, and that God would deliver them from the latter and give them a place in the former: I have said they believed, but I modify by saying, they hoped against hope. All was shrouded in darkness and uncertainty. They lived under an impenetrable cloud, that portended scarcely aught but destruction in death.

I submit that Nature and Reason never will have a better opportunity to manifest their revealing power than in the golden age of Greece and Rome. Those great philosophers thought seriously and honestly on all great subjects, and therefore we find here the most splendid illustration of what may be known of divine and spiritual things, apart from the Bible. Now, honor bright, where is the

Christian child of five summers who could afford to exchange knowledge with these great ones, on almost all the subjects reviewed above? The question makes us shudder, and we cry aloud, *nowhere, nowhere.*

Enumerating a number of topics at another place, I averred that some knowledge on all these is necessary to satisfy our ever-active mind, and to perfect our life.

Having observed, also, that Nature and Reason cannot furnish satisfactory answers to these problems, we have the true premises out of which to draw the imperative conclusion: That God will reveal to man all he ought to know on all matters otherwise "too high for him."

Can God do this? Certainly he can. How? You shall see.

THE POSSIBILITY AND METHOD OF REVELATION.

God is All-wise and All-powerful. "Nothing is impossible with Him." This means of course, that nothing is impossible with Him that is not inconsistent with His moral attributes, or with the nature and constitution of things. Neither of these is implied in a divine revelation to man. Created in the image of God pre-supposes that man's mind is

so constituted that God can impress ideas upon
him when and where He will. Indeed, man was
mentally constituted to such an end; for it is
reasonable to believe that God purposed to lead
man upward and onward into higher and still
higher realms of knowledge, eternally. We do
not understand the exact *modus operandi* by which
such ideas are impressed upon the mind, but
neither do we know how we get any other knowledge. It is true that we know something of the
faculties of the mind, and the laws of thought; but
there is an inner holy of holies into which no
human priest has entered, and touching which
man's *knowledge is ignorance.* Yes, surely God
can impart knowledge to His rational creatures.

The method of revelation adopted by God was to
inspire holy men to speak and write His thoughts
and will. I have said, "speak" and "write,"
purposely; for while God's word to us is written,
we do not forget that a great deal was spoken under the guidance and motions of the Holy Ghost,
which was never committed to writing. Now all
that we need to know, and all that future nations
need to know, is contained in our Scripture; but .
the prophets, Jesus Christ, and the apostles delivered many messages and performed many miracles

which we may suppose had a purely local application and mission. I believe all that which was of universal application and edification was written down, either directly by those to whom the revelation was originally made, or by those who were divinely commissioned and inspired to act in the capacity of author or scribe.

This brings me to say that God's word to the world is not oral, but written. Why this should be so is manifest from a few considerations. I cannot do better than to quote here the arguments adduced by eminent writers, as found in Horne's Introduction:

1. Oral Tradition is so uncertain and so insecure a guide, that if a revelation claiming to be divine be not transmitted by writing, it cannot possibly be preserved in its purity, or serve mankind as a certain rule of faith and of life. In illustration of this remark we may observe that writing is a more secure method of conveyance than tradition, being neither so liable to involuntary mistakes, through weakness of memory or understanding, nor so subject to voluntary falsifications, suppressions, additions, either out of malice or design. It is also a method of conveyance more natural and human. It is nothing extraordinary for a book to

be transmitted pure and entire from generation to
generation; but a traditionary doctrine, especially
if it be of any considerable length, cannot be preserved without a miracle, without the occasional
interposition of Almighty God to renew the
memory of it at particular intervals, or His con-
tinual assistance and inspiration to keep it always
alive and vigorous. It is likewise a method more
complete and uniform, presenting itself to all at
once and to all alike, to be compared together;
whereas a traditionary doctrine must be communicated little by little, and without doubt communicated differently at different times by different persons. It is, moreover, a method of conveyance
more general and diffusive. A man's writings
reach further than his words; and surely we need
not observe that it is the practice of mankind,
when they would publish anything, to have it written or printed in a book.

2. Experience shows that writing is a method of
conveyance more lasting than tradition.

It is an old and trite saying that a word perishes,
but a letter written remains. Jesus Christ is said
to have performed many other miracles, and to
have done many other memorable things, besides
those which have been committed to writing; but,

observe how much more faithful record is than
mere report—the few, comparatively speaking,
which were written are preserved and credited,
while the many, which were not recorded in writing, have long since been utterly lost and forgotten.
Everything of any consequence we desire to have
in writing. By this, laws are promulgated; by
this, arts and sciences are propagated; by this,
titles and estates are secured. What do we know
of ancient history but the little that comes down to
us in books and writings? Tradition passes away
like a moving cloud; but books may live as long as
the sun and moon endure.

3. To the preceding arguments we may add, that
it is certainly more fair and open, more free from
suspicion of any fraud or contrivance, to have a religion preserved in writing, to be read and exam-
ined by all, than to have it left only with a few,
to be by them communicated in discourse to others,
as no two persons express the same thing exactly
in the same manner, nor even the same person at
different times.

The heathen philosophers had their *exoteric*
and *esoteric* doctrines, as they distinguish them,
that is, some which they generally delivered and
some which they communicated only to a few

select auditors; but the first propagators of Christianity, knowing no such distinction, delivered the whole doctrine which they professed. to have received from the Lord. The heathen priests had their mysteries, which they concealed from the profane and vulgar; but Christianity can never be made too public. Most other religions also are committed to writing for their professors, and it would be a prejudice to the Christian religion if it did not enjoy the same advantage. The Jews had what they called an oral law, a well as a written one; and the one, as well as the other, they asserted to have been given by God on Mount Sinai—the oral to serve as a comment or explanation of the written law. But, in process of time, these traditions multiplied so rapidly that the Jews found it necessary to keep their traditions no longer as traditions, but committed them to writing, and they are now preserved in the books called the Talmud. So fallible is tradition, so secure is writing, even in the opinion of the greatest traditionists; and if the doctrines of religion must one time or other be written, it is better surely to have them written by inspired authors at first than by others afterwards.

4. Lastly, the importance of the matter, the variety of the subjects, and the design of the institu-

tions, contained in those books which Jews and
Christians account sacred, are additional reasons
why they should be committed to writing.   The
matter is of no less importance than the whole will
of God and the salvation of mankind, our duty
here and our happiness hereafter; and if anything
deserves to be written, do not these things deserve
to be recorded in the most lasting characters?
The subjects, likewise, are very various—histories
of times past and prophecies of things to come, ora-
tions and epistles, sublime points of faith and plain
rules of practice, hymns and prayers and thanks-
givings, too excellent to be forgotten, but too many
to be remembered.   The Law was for a single
nation, but the Gospel is for the whole world.
For a single nation it was requisite that their laws
should be written, or to what can they appeal, and
by what can they regulate their practice?   If it was
necessary for their law to be written, it was certainly much more necessary for the Gospel, which
was designed to be both of perpetual and universal
obligation, a religion for all ages and all times.

The Holy Scripture in our possession is divine.
"Holy men wrote as they were moved by the Holy
Ghost."   "All Scripture is given by inspiration."
It is however in point to say that while "all Scrip-

ture is given by inspiration," not all we have in
the Bible was revealed by God, nor is every word
the word of God, strictly speaking. The Bible, in
fact, contains the words of Satan, of bad men, of
good men, and of angels, as well as those of God.
Again, it is very obvious that a very great deal in
the Bible was known by the authors through the
various ways in which knowledge is gained. History, observation and experience, for example;
were brought into requisition. Whatever they
could know through ordinary intelligence, they
were divinely guided to appropriate. Everything
beyond this point was directly revealed. Such
revelation was made through dreams, visions, and
audible words, Urim and Thummim, external
signs, and sometimes by inward suggestion.

I wish you to bear in mind, however, that every
portion of the sacred Scriptures is inspired. I do
not believe that those who spoke and wrote were
machines, or passive agents in the hand of the
Spirit—that the Spirit broke down, so to speak, the
fixed laws of thought and of language—but that He
honored and spoke according to them. I believe
that those who spoke and wrote did so in full
possession of their individual peculiarities. In expressing the "doctrines of God," they used their

own words and idioms. In writing "the form of sound words," they were indeed kept from error in essentials: history, doctrine, precepts, laws, etc., but not in non-essentials: grammar, rhetoric, style, etc. The former is the divine side of the Bible, pre-eminently; the latter the human side, pre-eminently. In the light of this view, accordingly, we can easily reconcile the little discrepancies which are found in the sacred pages.

In the sixty-six books of the Bible, written by about forty different men during a period of some fifteen hundred years, we hear the Voice of God to the human race; there is not a faculty of the mind, an aspiration of the soul, a feeling of the heart in the realm of the spiritual, that is not met and satisfied by this Book. It does not only bring knowledge, but it is also a blessed means of grace; for it is the Holy Spirit's vehicle in bringing "life and immortality to light" in our souls.

This Divine Revelation is one of the three means of grace in the Church, and is profitable for doctrine, for reproof, for correction, for instruction in righteousness, that the man of God may be perfected, thoroughly furnished unto all good works.

May this Word have free course, run and be glorified. Amen.

" A glory gilds the sacred page,
    Majestic like the sun;
  It gives a light to every age,
    It gives—but borrows none.

"The hand that gave it still supplies
    The gracious light and heat ;
  His truths upon the nations rise,
    They rise, but never set.

"Let everlasting thanks be Thine,
    For such a bright display,
  As makes a world of darkness shine
    With beams of heavenly day.

"My soul rejoices to pursue
    The steps of Him I love,
  Till glory breaks upon my view
    In brighter worlds above."

LECTURE VIII.

SACRAMENT OF BAPTISM.

JOHN iii. 5.

John iii. 5. Verily, verily, I say unto thee, except a man be born of water and of the Spirit, he cannot enter into the kingdom of God.

LECTURE VIII.

HOLY Baptism is one of the two Sacraments, and one of the three means of grace in the Church.

Christian Baptism strikes its roots into ancient laws and customs. It is a well-known fact that long before the advent of our Lord, this rite was practiced by many or all the heathen nations. With them it had no other signification than the mere washing away and cleansing of external impurities. The Israelites, also, in obedience to a law on the subject, practiced this ceremony, primarily for the same purpose as that of the Gentiles, but also as a symbol of purification from sin, and an initiation into the worship of God. If we may credit the Talmud, we are led to believe that the Hebrews baptized all the proselytes, circumcised and uncircumcised alike. Some writers think that this rite of the Israelites had its origin in the act of Jacob, as recorded in Gen. xxxv. 2. About this, however, we need not to be concerned, for the only point to be scored here is, that baptism, after

some fashion, was observed by the nations in ancient times. This fact, it is very obvious, supplies
the ground for Christian Baptism. It is a significant truth that all Israel looked for the rite of baptism to be established when the Messiah should
come. It was well known that on His appearing
many changes would be effected; that matters in
general would be revolutionized; and, in view of
this belief, they seemed to expect this Sacrament
to be practiced.

Now when John the Baptist comes on the scene,
preaching baptism and repentance, all the people
flock to hear him and to be baptized. Even the
proud and self-righteous present themselves, so that
John is forced to say: "Generation of vipers, who
hath warned you to flee from the wrath to come."
From the Baptist's mission and work the conclusion is inevitable that if baptism had been a
new thing—an innovation—it would have been
utterly rejected; but being practiced before, and
expected to accompany the new order of things, it
was cheerfully accepted.

In this view of things, we perceive that Holy
Baptism, as instituted by the command of Christ,
is an old ceremony on its external and material
side, but a new Sacrament on its spiritual side, in

meaning, scope and effect. In this, as everywhere else, we observe how the new dispensation was rooted and grounded in the old.

In answer to the question, What is the difference between John's baptism and that of Christ? I may venture to say, None. This answer is justified by the fact that John exhorted all who applied for baptism to repent of their sins, and believe on the expected Messiah. When Christ came forward to claim that title, John made haste to direct all who were, or were about to be, baptized, to Christ, and thereby completed his mission as forerunner; and therein did their baptism find its real significance and effect.

Another justification lies in the fact that the early Christian Church regarded the two baptisms as the same. All the disciples of John who professed faith in Christ as the Messiah, were not baptized the second time. The baptism of John sufficed. Those only who did not at first thus acknowledge Christ, but received the baptism of John in an entirely different sense, were afterwards rebaptized with the baptism of Christ. History teaches that many false disciples of John continued to baptize into the coming Messiah, rejecting Christ as the Messiah; so that afterward when any such accepted Christ, they were properly rebaptized.

In the light of these historic facts, the only intelligent conclusion is, that the two rites were
practically identical.

CHRISTIAN BAPTISM.

Proceeding now to consider Christian Baptism,
I desire to somewhat rapidly sketch some of its
distinctive features.

*First comes the command by Christ that it shall
be a universal Sacrament.*

The disciples were commanded to go forth everywhere to make disciples and to baptize. "Go ye
and make disciples of all nations, baptizing them
in the name of the Father and of the Son and of
the Holy Ghost." "Preach the gospel to every
creature," "He that believeth and is baptized
shall be saved." This great commission couples
salvation and baptism. The context shows, it is
true, that such connection is not absolute, but elec-
tive. In any case where this Sacrament cannot
possibly be administered, we may well believe
that God can save without it; but in all ordinary
circumstances the command and the observance
is absolute. The Church marches forward to the
conquest of all nations with the Bible, the Holy
Baptism and the Holy Supper in her right hand.

These are all the weapons she carries, but with these she is certain of complete triumph.

Baptism must be administered in the name of the Holy Trinity.

This is at once a confession of the triune God, Father, Son and Holy Ghost, and of the fact that the three Persons in the Godhead are equally interested and engaged in our salvation. "God so loved the world that He gave His only begotten Son that whosoever believeth in Him should not perish, but have eternal life." "If any man sin, we have an advocate with the Father, even Jesus Christ the righteous, who hath made propitiation for our sins, and not for ours only, but also for the whole world." "Verily, verily, I say unto thee, except a man be born of water and of the Spirit, he cannot enter into the kingdom of God." Many other texts bring out the same truth.

The persons authorized to administer this Sacrament are the ordained ministers of the Church.

By virtue of their office in the kingdom of Christ, it is incumbent on them to act for the 'King in placing His seal upon all those who are becoming His subjects. There are those who maintain that in extraordinary circumstances a layman or a parent may properly administer this means of

grace. This I consider as doubtful. While it
must be emphasized that Baptism in the hand of
the minister is not used like a wand in the magi-
cian's hand to effect a magic phenomenon, nevertheless, our Lord ordains that His ambassadors shall be
the ministers of this mystery, and that ends all
controversy.

*The substance of Baptism is both material and
divine.*

The material element is water, the divine,
Christ's word and promise. "Baptism is not mere
water, but it is that water which is connected with
God's word, which says: 'Go ye into all the world
and preach the Gospel to every creature: he that
believeth and is baptized shall be saved, but he that
believeth not shall be damned.'" If baptism is not
mere water, neither is it mere word and promise.
Just as the water must be connected with God's
word, so also must the word be connected with the
water. In other words, there is here a mutual connection and union. The reason why this matter
must be emphasized is this: there are those who
think so lightly and superficially on this subject
that they are not backward to declare that instead
of water, another element may be used, or even no
material element at all—that the bare baptismal for-

mula is sufficient. I do not believe this. I have all
confidence in the power of God's word to effect a
new life in the soul, but I insist that the repetition
of the formula of baptism, without water, is not
baptism. Our Lord united the two—water and the
word—and "what God hath joined together, let not
man put asunder." We may not know all the reasons why the material side of the sacrament is
water, but some of the reasons seem to be obvious.
In the first place, man is so constituted that he
loves to deal with the concrete and tangible.
Truth presented in the abstract can, of course, be
understood and accepted; but if that truth can also
be shown in the concrete, it makes a more vivid,
and, frequently, a more intelligent impression upon
the persons for whom it is intended. It is a well-
established fact that things that are seen and heard
and felt, etc., are never forgot, while those that are
abstractly conceived are soon in oblivion. This is
especially true of the young and unlearned.

In the light of the above, there is a striking and
beautiful propriety in Holy Baptism. *It is a poem
in water. It is an object lesson.* The abstract
truths of Regeneration and Sanctification are presented to man in material forms. Just as water
applied to the body cleanses and purifies it, so does

the Holy Spirit regenerate and sanctify the soul. As no other element is used for common washings and lustrations, so may there be no other element substituted for water in baptism. Furthermore, just as certainly as the material element is present in the sacrament, so certainly is the divine element present, the Holy Ghost. It is right here that endless comfort is afforded to those who receive this sacrament, as well as to parents and sponsors who hereby dedicate their children and wards to God. They have the unceasing assurance that by virtue of their baptism the Spirit is vouchsafed to them, who will, if unresisted, perfect God's work within them.

But while baptism gives assurance of the gift of the Holy Ghost, to cleanse and purify the soul, it is also a perpetual reminder of the duty of the person baptized. Luther's catechism fitly teaches: "Water baptism signifies that the old man should be drowned and destroyed by daily sorrow and repentance, and that a new man should daily arise that shall dwell in the presence of God." This symbolical teaching of baptism doubtless finds its meaning chiefly in immersion, but it does show forth very strikingly what the subject of baptism must do.

From this last paragraph it must by no means be understood that I lay the main stress on the symbolical signification of the subject under consideration. This is precisely what all anabaptists do, but I am not their mouth-piece. *I believe and declare that it must be regarded as a means of grace, first, last and all the time.* In it the triune God conveys grace to the heart, and also causes it to stand as a perpetual sign and seal of that grace.

Touching the mode, two may be mentioned, affusion and immersion. Either and both of these modes are perfectly valid. The efficacy of this sacrament does not at all depend on the mode or administration, but on the substance. The latter belongs to the essential, the former to the *adiaphora*. Those who practice affusion, proceed on the ground of expedience in administration *ana means of grace as to substance;* while those who immerse, proceed on the ground of essentiality of mode in administration, *and symbolism as to substance.* The former is a striking evidence of the magnification of the substance and end of baptism, while the latter is just as striking for magnifying the mere ceremony or human adjunct. But while men may pin their faith to mode, God, thanks be to His name, is willing to fulfill the engagement into which He enters thereby.

SUBJECTS OF BAPTISM.

The subjects of baptism are adults and children.

No one disputes the first mentioned class. Romanists and Protestants, anabaptists and pedo-baptists, alike agree at this point.

Relative to the second class, there is disagreement now and for a long time past. Why there should be it is very hard to understand; but it must be owing, not to lack of conscientiousness, but to stubborn prejudice born of partisan training, and in some instances, of mental obtuseness. That infants are proper subjects for this sacrament is so obvious that it ought to commend itself to every Christian.

Allow me to mention some of the arguments upon which the foregoing assertion is based.

First. Children belonged to the Old Testament dispensation.

At Gen. xvii. 9–14, we have the following positive command: "And God said unto Abraham, thou shalt keep my covenant therefore, thou, and thy seed after thee in their generations. This is my covenant which ye shall keep between me and

---

thee and thy seed after thee: Every man child among you shall be circumcised. And ye shall circumcise the flesh of your foreskin; and it shall be a token of the covenant betwixt me and you." This command stipulates and recognizes their relation to the Church. Hereby they are brought into covenant relation with God, by which covenant God conferred on the children equal blessings with the adults. That the rite of circumcision was observed throughout the entire Old Testament Church to the time of Christ is, of course, admitted by all. Christ Himself, being born under the law, was circumcised on the eighth day, being called Jesus.

Now it cannot be said that this was all true touching the old dispensation, but that under the Gospel dispensation matters have taken another turn, for the reason that a new element or condition has been introduced into it, viz., faith. This is simply not true, for although the old dispensation was primarily of law—to lead them to Christ—nevertheless salvation was not by the fulfilling of the law, but by faith in the promised Messiah. Every foreshadowing and promise of this Saviour was the Gospel from which it is clear that it had its beginning, not with the advent of

Christ, but literally with the very first announcement and promise of His advent, immediately after the Fall. Every succeeding covenant which God made with man was therefore a proclamation of the Gospel. Now this fact is most strikingly proved by words from the mouth of the Apostle Paul (Gal. iii. 6, vii. 8), where he declares that God's covenant with Abraham, the very one embracing the circumcision of all the male children, was the Gospel, and therefore involved the element of faith. Hear him: "Even as Abraham believed God, and it was accounted unto him for righteousness. Know ye therefore that they which are of faith, the same are the children of Abraham. And the Scripture, foreseeing that God would justify the heathen through faith, preached before the Gospel to Abraham, saying, In thee shall all the nations of the earth be blessed." When Christ came, in view of whom the covenant with Abraham was made and which constituted the Gospel to Abraham, did He fulfill or abrogate the covenant? This question can surely have but one answer, and that is, that He fulfilled it. Otherwise He came to abrogate the Gospel, and that would mean that He destroyed what it was the purpose of God He should confirm and establish. It means, therefore, that

we are to-day without the Gospel. All this is
fallacious on its very face. But if He came to
fulfill the Old Covenant or Gospel, then He necessarily and absolutely continued the same parties to
that Covenant, God on the one side, and all the
nations of the earth, adults and children, on the
other. For remember, the promise was to Abraham
and his seed, and to all who became the spiritual
children of Abraham.

It is self-evident that if God desires to change the
rite and ceremony of admission into this covenant
at any time, He is at liberty to do so, for this does
not affect the covenant itself. At a certain period
of the world's history, God's wisdom may see that
this initiatory rite may be so changed that it will
teach, symbollically, new ideas and conceptions.
Christian baptism is thus made to take the place,
as a rite of initiation and means of grace, of circumcision in the old dispensation.

In concluding this part of the subject I cannot
do better than to quote the words of Dr. N. L.
Rice: "Since the children of believers were put
into the Church by the positive law of God, they
can be put out only by the positive law of God. Inference will not answer the purpose. You cannot
infer men out of their political rights. Men do not

reason so infallibly that we may safely trust our
rights and privileges to their deductions and infer-
ences. I enjoy the rights of a citizen of these
United States by the plain letter of the constitution. If you wish to deprive me of these rights,
you must prove that the constitution has been so
altered as to exclude me. You must, to deprive
me of any political rights, find law as positive, and
of as high authority, as that which originally conferred them. This principle holds equally good
in ecclesiastical matters. If I prove that God put
certain persons into his Church, you cannot exclude
them unless you can point to the law authorizing
you to do so. God did put the children of believ- ,
ers into His Church by clear and positive command,
and you cannot exclude them except by law equally
clear and positive. The law of command including children in His Church is plain and undeni-
able, but I challenge any one to show a law or command excluding them, coming either from Christ
or the Apostles. All this shows most conclusively
that infant Church membership spreads its roots
into the love and tender mercy of God to children,
as anciently displayed; and since God is unchange-
able, He cannot turn against our children in these
modern days!''

Second. Children have a right to baptism by the invitation of Christ.

Certain mothers brought their children to Christ that He should put His hands on them and bless them. The disciples rebuked these mothers, but Christ was much displeased, and said: "Let little children come unto me, and forbid them not, for of such is the kingdom of God." Now notice three things. First, the phrase "kingdom of God" is admitted on all sides to mean God's kingdom and reign on earth—the Church. "For of such is the kingdom of God," hence, is equivalent to saying, for of such is the Church. This is understood as meaning, these children have fitness for a place in the Church, and, therefore, do not push them away from Me; let them come, I will bless them. Secondly, baptism is the divinely authorized right of initiation into the Church. "Verily, verily, I say unto thee, except a man be born of water and of the Spirit, he cannot enter the kingdom of God." Placing side by side the fact that baptism is the door to the Church and the Saviour's declaration that "of such is the kingdom of God," there can simply be no mistaking the will of the Master relative to the relation of children to the Church and to baptism.

Third. Children are included in the many family baptisms recorded in the New Testament.

I mention the case of "Cornelius's house," Acts x. In the 16th chapter of Acts, there is mention made of "Lydia and her household." In this same chapter, the baptism of the "Philippian jailer and his house" is recorded. The baptism of "Crispus and his house" is narrated in Acts xviii. In 1 Cor. i. 16 Paul writes that he "baptized the household of Stephanas."

Surely, if the terms "house" and "household" mean anything, they mean the families of the persons indicated in the record. I do not think that this has ever been denied. This signifies the inclusion of children. But opposers of infant baptism object by declaring that all the members of these families were adults. The drowning man grasps at a straw, and just as senseless and desperate are many people in their interpretation of the Scriptures—especially if they have a lame theory to defend. If the sacred record made mention of but a single household baptism, there would be room for the position that all the members thereof were adults; but since a number of families are named, that attitude becomes untenable. To say the very least, it would be marvelous if none of

these households embraced youths and children,
seeing that such is always the case in the common
course of family life where there are a number of
members.	It is not without point to remark that
it is by no means likely that we have a record of
more than a small fraction of the household bap-
tisms performed by the disciples.	Probably there
were hundreds of such; but because it would not
be for our spiritual edification to have them nar-
rated, they were passed over.	Now this consider-
ation confirms the pedo-baptist position, render-
ing it simply impregnable.	I say it frankly, and
after due thought, that it would be just as easy for
me to oppose the Sacrament of Christian baptism,
as founded in the Scriptures, as to oppose infant
baptism, seeing that it is equally Scriptural.

*Fourth. The voice of history pleads emphatically
for infant baptism.*

Every student of history will, of course, not deny
that this has been the practice for at least fifteen
centuries.	Luther, Calvin, and Zwingli, during
the Reformation days, all practiced it.	So have
the great majority of all the Protestant denomina-
tions: the Lutheran, the Mother Church of all
Protestant daughters, with her forty-five millions
of members; the Church of England, the Presby-

13

terian, the Methodist, with each their millions; together with all the other branches of the Church
of Christ, with their additional millions. The
Baptist species alone, embracing not more than
an insignificant fraction of Christendom, raises a
dissenting voice—one defective note in the glorious
diapason.

For a thousand years before the Reformation,
infant baptism was almost the universal practice.
But the cry goes up, "Yes, that is true, but then
the Church was corrupt—she had departed from
the 'good old ways' of the Church Fathers—things
were different then." Let us see.

The greatest defender of the faith at the close of
the fourth century was Augustine. His acute and
learned opponent was Pelagius. The latter was
born about the middle of the fourth century, and
besides ample natural endowment of mind, he was
well informed, the result, very largely, of travels
and observations. Pelagius traversed through all
the various countries of Christendom. Now, the
heresies which he put forth so vigorously but honestly, biased him against the doctrine of infant
baptism, not in heart, perhaps, but in mind; for it
stood stoutly in the way of some of his theological
opinions. In view of this fact his testimony is

doubly strong. What is that testimony? This, viz., "I have never heard of even any impious heretics who claim that infants should not be baptized." Again, "Who can be so impious as to deny baptism to infants?" Let this witness, among the many who might be adduced, suffice for this period. The great and pious Church father, Cyprian, born about the year two hundred, and bishop of the city of Carthage, in answer to Fidus as to whether children ought to be baptized before they were eight days old, declares as follows, as the mouthpiece of a council that was held at Carthage to deliberate upon this very subject: "Cyprian, and the rest of the bishops who were present in the Council, sixty-six in number, to Fidus our brother. As to the case of infants: Whereas you believe they ought not to be baptized inside of two or three days after they are born, and that the rule of circumcision is to be observed, that no one should be baptized before the eighth day after his birth; we are all of us of a different opinion. As to your opinion, no one was of your mind, but we all hold that the mercy and grace of God—through baptism—should not be withheld from any one that is born. This, therefore, dear brother, was our conclusion in the Council, that we ought not to hinder any person from baptism and the grace of God, whose mercy and kindness is extended to all of us." This deliverance was made about one hundred and fifty years after the death of Saint John, and has, hence, singular significance. About eighty-five years after the death of the Apostle above mentioned, Origen saw the light of day. This man was a prince among human kind in his day. It is said that if the New Testament should be lost, it could be reproduced from the writings of this Father, so extensive and thorough are his quotations from the Scriptures. Let Origen speak on the subject in hand: "According to the usage of the Church, baptism is given even to infants, when if there were nothing in infants that need forgiveness and mercy, the grace of baptism would not seem to be necessary." Again, "infants are baptized for the remission of sins." Again, "for this cause it was that the Church received an order from the apostles to give baptism to infants."

Only one more witness, and the case will rest. Justin Martyr was born in the last quarter of the first century. If he did not himself see the apostle John, he was at least a disciple of those who were disciples of John. What does he say? Of those who were members of the Christian Church he writes: "A part of them were sixty or seventy years old, who were made disciples of Christ from their infancy. Baptism, without controversy, is now and always has been the initiatory rite into discipleship." The only rational inference, accordingly, is that Justin Martyr has reference here to Christian baptism. This, indeed, is the only sense in which the words "disciple" and "infancy" square: any other meaning causes a contradiction in terms.

I have only now to say that under the tutorship of the Church and apostolic Fathers above named, one must be strikingly obtuse and stubborn to reject the unanimous verdict in favor of infant baptism. The chorus is full-voiced and all the parts harmonize on this subject. Who will resist the inevitable? *Verily, infant baptism has come down to us with the sign and seal of history and of the Scriptures upon it, and so it may well be, as it is, the door to the Church for old and young alike.*

Leaving the topic of "subjects of baptism," I proceed to take up the last in this lecture, to wit,

THE BENEFITS OF BAPTISM.

I shall limit myself to a very few words. Christ

said to Nicodemus, "Except a man be born of
water and of the Spirit, he cannot enter into the
kingdom of God." Paul declares: "Baptism is
the laver of regeneration and the renewing of the
Holy Ghost."

Since baptism is the only door to the Church, it
is very obvious that this Sacrament confers an unspeakable benefit in admitting the subject to her
blessings and her privileges. Ordinarily, there is
no salvation apart from her sacred precincts, within
which are all the saving means of grace. To obtain access, therefore, to these means, by which
man comes into fellowship with saints and with
God, is a blessing as great as heaven. But this is
only one benefit. Before sinful man comes into
such intimate relationship with his God and
Father, there must be at least the beginning of a
new life. "Ye must be born again." "Born of
the Spirit." "That which is born of the flesh is
flesh, but that which is born of the Spirit is
spirit."

*The new birth takes place through the medium of
either of two means, the Holy Scriptures or Baptism.*

The first is the authorized means for adults; the
latter for infants. Both means are the vehicle of

the Holy Ghost, and it is the Holy Ghost who cre-
ates anew.   In the case of adults, intelligence and
voluntary choice are implied, and hence the Scriptures, offering life or death, are the appropriate instrument of the Spirit.   With them regeneration
is demanded before baptism is permitted.   To them,
whatever else it may be, baptism is a sign and
seal of what has already taken place through the
Word, besides formally introducing them to the
higher mysteries of godliness.

In the case of infants, knowledge and choice are
not existent; but, needing a new heart as well as
adults, holy baptism has been instituted as the
means for doing what the written Scriptures do in
the case of adults.   Personally, I do not believe
that regeneration is identical in infants and adults.
The former have nothing but natural depravity;
or, as I prefer, *spiritual death.*   The latter are also
guilty of actual sin, *or spiritual death intensified
by personal act.*   The former have *inherited* their
condition, and which is nothing but *simple death.*
The latter are guilty of *voluntarily developing this
simple death into deeper death,* and therefore to
this *aggravated death,* which is totally subjective,
there is superadded *sin against God.   In my view
there is well-nigh and infinite distance between the*

simple spiritual death of the babe and the aggra-
vated condition of the willing sinner. Accordingly,
the Spirit's mission in the case of the babe is nothing more than to bring spiritual life—which I shall
explain further at another place—and that without
the babe's knowledge and consent, inasmuch as
knowledge and consent were not involved in its
death. This God bestows upon the infant purely
for Christ's sake. The adult having literally
sinned, and under the light of knowledge and by
personal choice, the Spirit's mission is to regenerate him with his knowledge and consent.

In this view of things the long drawn-out discussion concerning the necessity of faith for a valid
and efficacious reception of baptism is all at the
end of the word—*palaver.* Such discussion does
not recognize a distinction between things that
differ; it indicates a signal confusion of ideas.

More of this under the subject of "Regeneration."

From all that has been said in this lecture relative to the Sacrament of Baptism, the inevitable
conclusion forces itself upon us that it is a most
divine and heavenly institution, and that the only
alternative open to man is to use and appropriate
it, to his endless weal and comfort.

LECTURE IX.

THE SACRAMENT OF THE ALTAR.

1 Cor. x. 16.

1 Cor. x. *16.* The bread which we break, is it not the communion of the body of Christ? The cup of blessing which we bless, is it not the communion of the blood of Christ?

LECTURE IX.

THE second Sacrament, and the third means of grace is variously called the Lord's Supper, the Eucharist, the Holy Communion, and, by the Reformers, the Sacrament of the Altar. Discussion has been rife over the true intent and meaning of the words of the institution, all Protestants agreeing as against Romanists, but disagreeing among themselves.

In this Sacrament, as in that of Baptism, there are two parts—the material and the divine. The material is bread and wine; the divine, the body and blood of Christ. These two parts are reciprocally united to each other in the sacrament; neither is present without the other in every properly consecrated and administered communion. This is a great mystery, but it is according to the will of God as taught in Holy Writ.

As Baptism takes the place of Circumcision, so, also, does the Holy Supper take the place of the Passover. As the Sacrificial lamb was eaten by

those in the Old Testament Dispensation at the
Passover Feast, so do those in the New Dispensation at the Communion Feast partake of the body
and blood of Christ, the Lamb of God. Thus
Baptism and the Lord's Supper alike have their
roots and foundations in the old economy. After
these preliminary remarks, I call your attention to
the Scriptural meaning and purport of the words
of the institution.

MEANING AND PURPORT.

Like every other matter, this blessed means of
grace was covered over by a heap of Romish error
at and before the Reformation era. I will not stop
to rehearse all the errors and corruptions, but suffice it to say that the one that claims our attention
in this connection is that of Transubstantiation.
Rome taught that at the time of the consecration
of the elements—bread and wine—the bread is
transmuted into the body of Christ, and the wine
into the blood of Christ. These material elements
are no longer such in essence, but only in form.
Eating and drinking, therefore, at the Sacramental
Table, meant nothing short of the oral mastication
and deglutition of the body and blood of Christ.

The Reformers unite in declaring this theory a

manifest error, unauthorized by Scripture, and un-
supported by the senses and by reason. Of course,
the question is not whether such a thing were possible with God, but whether the words of the institution justify the theory, as also sound reason and
the senses.

The answer is, they do not. The words of the
institution plainly declare the bread and wine to be
still bread and wine after the consecration. Listen:
"As oft as ye eat this bread and drink this cup ye
do show the Lord's death till He come." In this
there is not one jot or tittle to even intimate that a
change is effected in the elements. On the other
hand, these words clearly teach the unchanged and
natural constitution of them.

To the above may be added the testimony of the
senses, which, it is true, are not always to be depended on, especially in their testimony touching
spiritual things; nevertheless, as circumstantial
witnesses, they ought to be admitted into court.
There are four of these testifying concerning the
subject in hand. They are sight, smell, taste and
touch. These are unanimous in affirming that
the bread and wine in the Supper retain their natural and original phenomena; and upon such data,
the reason decides that the substance or essence

producing the phenomena must be natural and
original—that is, that the material elements are
literally bread and wine. Place this testimony by
the side of the Word, and the conclusion is irrever-
sible that no transubstantiation has occurred, and
that the whole thing is a fabrication.

Another error is covered by the terms "Con-
substantiation," "Impanation," "Subpanation."
These words are meant to express the notion that
the body and blood of Christ are somehow locally
included in the bread and wine, and partaken by
the communicants.   Protestants have charged each
other with holding this view; especially has the
Lutheran Church been thus charged.   The Lutheran Church, however, boldly and persistently re-
pels this stigma upon her fair name, and rightfully
challenges the whole theological world to prove a
single instance where any of her leaders have ever
taught such doctrines.   She does hold to the real
presence of the Lord in the Supper, but not by
local inclusion.   She repudiates every term which
is designed to convey such an idea.

Another misinterpretation of the words of the
institution by Christ, is the doctrine of the merely
symbolical import of the Communion.   This view
is sometimes called the Emblematic.

This doctrine entirely discards the presence of the body and blood of Christ, and hence holds that the visible elements are nothing but emblems or symbols of the absent Christ. That as a rite it is only commemorative, and not a distinctive means of grace. Christ is received in the Supper, but only as He is received by the hearing and believing of the Word under ordinary circumstances. This view is based on the position that the verb "is" in the institution means to "signify," "represents" or "symbolizes" the "body" and "blood" there distributed and received—and herein lies the fallacy.

Again, the view is held by a large body of Christians that the Eucharist is truly much more than a commemorative ceremony; that it is a precious Sacrament and means of grace; that the glorified body and blood of Christ are enjoyed by the participant. This body and blood being locally present in heaven, cannot be also in the Sacrament at the same time. Therefore the only mode of reception of Christ, and feeding upon Him, is by faith. The body and blood of Christ are not presented and received in, with or under the bread and wine, but these physical elements merely excite faith in the Saviour, by which He is

appropriated, and incorporated into the communicant's life.

Now concerning the last two views, which are
in many respects much more acceptable to most
minds than the preceding ones, the question may
well be asked, What particular benefit does the
Lord's Supper confer that the Christian does not
already enjoy, apart from it? Or, what distinctive
significance does this Sacrament have?

By permission of the author, Dr. J. G. Morris, I
avail myself of a lengthy extract from a very
learned and exhaustive article on this subject, in
the *Lutheran Quarterly* for April, 1883.

He writes:

"Nor do we believe that the presence of Christ
consists in a mere figurative representation, that
is, that the bread only represents or signifies His
body and that the wine only represents or signifies
his blood.

"This view is opposed to the language of the
institution. It does not say, Take, eat, this represents my body or is a sign of it (and so of the
wine), but it speaks of an actual, real and true
existence: 'This is my body;' 'this is my blood;'
that which only represents or signifies a thing, is
not the thing itself. Here Christ is speaking of

His body that was given for us, and of His blood that was shed for us, so that His language cannot be understood of a mere sign or of a figurative body and blood.

"This view is also contrary to the nature and character of the New Testament. True, in the Old Testament, the sacraments and sacrifices were "shadows and images" (signs) of "good things to come," Heb. x. 1; Col. ii. 17, but in the New Testament is the substance itself. Thus in the Old Testament, the Paschal lamb represented, signified, prefigured Christ, but in the New, Christ is really the Paschal Lamb, that was slain for our sins, 1 Cor. v. 7. If then, in the Holy Supper, these were nothing more than mere external signs of a covenant, there would be no difference between the Old and New Testaments, which, however, the Scriptures so distinctly specified. There would also be no difference between the Paschal lamb and the Holy Supper, whereas our Lord instituted it only after partaking of the Paschal lamb and thereby the latter was abolished ("finished") as a Sacrament of the Old Testament. On the contrary, in the Holy Supper as a Sacrament of the New Testament, necessarily something more is exhibited than a mere sign,

14

otherwise they would be the same thing, for we could not understand for what purpose Christ ordained and did not perpetuate that of the Paschal lamb. Of the latter, it could properly be said, This represents my body, but of the New Testament Sacrament it is said, This is my body. Indeed, the signs of the Old Testament, as such, would have been more expressive than those of the New. The slaying of the lamb "in the evening," the shedding of its blood, the preparation of it whole without a bone being broken, and the eating of it, accompanied with certain ceremonies, would have more impressively set forth the sufferings and death of Christ, than the bread and wine in the Holy Supper.

"If we interpret the words of Christ 'My body' to mean symbol of My body, then it follows that not His body, nor His blood, 'was given for us,' but a symbol of His body and blood, and hence we have a symbolical, and not a real atonement; in other words, Christ's death is no improvement of, or advance beyond, the sacrament of the Paschal lamb.

"Zwingli and his followers maintain that the word 'is' means represents, signifies, 'is a symbol of,' but learned men tell us that no translations of the Bible, ancient or modern, with any pretension to scholarly character, so render the word. No man whose authority is worth anything has ever dared to insert into the text of his translation, this is a symbol of his body. No impartial dictionary of the Greek assigns such a meaning to the word, except that of the rationalist, Schleusner, and that of the Zwinglian, Parkhurst, and these evidently had the design of promoting the false doctrine.* No good dictionary of the English, Hebrew, or, we may say, of any other language, gives such a meaning corresponding to the English verb 'to be,' or to the Greek equivalent verb.

"Some passages have been cited to prove that 'is' may mean 'is a symbol of,' for example, I am the door; I am the vine, ye are the branches; I am the bread of life. Thus Christ would say, 'I am the symbol of a door; I am the symbol of a vine; I am the symbol of bread,' which is absurd.

"In 1 Cor. x. 14, we have, 'That Rock was Christ;' the meaning of which is, that the real,

---

*Since writing the above, a Friend learned in Greek has informed me that the last edition of Liddell-Scott accords indeed to este, the meaning "signify," "import," but in an entirely different sense from "being an emblem or symbol of." The distinction may be readily seen from the illustration given, which, translated, is: "To say is to speak," *i. e.*, signifies to speak, but not as a symbol or emblem of speaking.

spiritual rock that went with the people was the
manifested Jehovah, that is, the Second Person of
the Trinity, Christ himself, in His pre-existent
state. So, when it is said that Christ is the door,
the vine, the bread, the foundation, the corner-
stone, etc., the resolution of the expression into
what is absolutely literal, turns not upon the word
'is,' but on the word 'door,' 'vine,' or other noun,
as the case may be.*

"Webster, in his dictionary, gives the fifth meaning to the word 'door'—means of approach—and
he quotes as proof that meaning: "I am the door,
by me if any man enter in, he shall be saved;' that
is, the word 'am' does not mean represent, signify,
or is a symbol of, but that Christ is really and
truly, not symbolically, the door; in other words,
He is the real means of approach to God. The
same reasoning is to be applied to the interpretation of the other words which Christ uses in de-
scribing His character.

"The dream language employed in the Old
Testament, as the three branches (are) three days,

<hr />

* "The substantive word 'is' connects the predicate with
the subject, and denotes that that which is offered in the Holy
Supper is really and truly not only bread, but also the body of
Christ."—*Schmid*.

Gen. xl. 12, the seven good kine (are) seven years, Gen. xli. 16, and others of similar import, cannot be successfully quoted against us.   1. The word are is not in the Hebrew text.   2. The branches, kine and ears, are not real branches, real kine, nor real ears, but the ideals of a dream. It is not three branches, but the three branches of the dream, that are three days.   3. Even if 'are' here meant signify, it would have no bearing on the Lord's Supper, which is not the interpretation of a dream.   4. The seven empty ears shall be seven years of famine, Gen. xli. 27.   Does that mean shall signify, as if they did not equally signify then? or does it mean that the empty ears, if we express what they really are to be, 'shall be seven years of famine.'   5. Would the inference be justifiable from this dream, that, Take, eat, these are seven ears prepared for your food—means, that there were no ears, but only symbols of ears?   Pluck and strip, these are branches covered with delicious fruit—does this mean that there were no branches, no fruit, but symbols of them?''   Who would thus interpret these words?—and it cannot be avoided, if you adopt the Zwinglian mode.*

---

* For a fuller discussion of this branch of the subject, see Krauth. Conserv. Reform., 613.

"Finally, the presence of the body and blood of Christ in the Lord's Supper, does not consist in a mere spiritual partaking of them as an act of faith.

"Now, we do not deny this spiritual partaking of Christ in itself, but on the contrary, we hold that no one can worthily partake of the Sacrament, who does not at the same time partake of Christ spiritually by faith. However, we must clearly distinguish between the worthy use and the real nature, or what we may call the substance, of this ordinance. For when we consider its nature and what is received by the communicant in it, we cannot be satisfied with regarding it as a mere spiritual reception, because our Lord gives us to eat and drink that which he presents in the Supper, so that in partaking of the bread and wine, we might at the same time really eat and drink His body and blood. He does not say, Take and believe, but, Eat and drink. The spiritual partaking of Christ can only be effected by faith, and believers alone can thus enjoy Him, but this can be done without the Sacrament. On the other hand, it is said of the unworthy and unbelieving, that they are guilty of the body and blood of Christ, because they do not discern the Lord's body. (As we shall have occasion to refer to this passage again, we shall pass by the further explanation of it for the present.)

"It necessarily follows from this, that the unworthy also partake of Christ's body and blood, though to their condemnation. We cannot otherwise conclude from Christ's words, that in them He included something more than that which believers of all ages—yea, even those of the Old Testament—enjoyed; otherwise, there would have been no necessity for a distinct institution. But we know that all believers, both of the Old and New Testaments, have at all times spiritually enjoyed or partaken of Christ by faith, as Paul expressly declares of the Israelites, 'that they drank of that spiritual rock that followed them, and that Rock was Christ, and that they did all eat of the spiritual meat and did all drink of the same spiritual drink,' 1 Cor. x. 34. If then there should be nothing more than a spiritual partaking, believers of the New Testament would be receiving nothing more than those of the Old; indeed, they would receive nothing more than they daily enjoy by faith, and hence such an institution as the Lord's Supper would be superfluous, if not fruitless, which would not be consistent with the wisdom and goodness of the divine Founder of this blessed ordinance.

"As we have now seen wherein the presence of the Lord in the Sacrament does not consist, it is necessary to consider the other side, and show,

"Secondly, What our Church really does hold to be true doctrine of Christ's presence in the Lord's Supper.

"Our Church confesses and believes in the true, essential presence of the body and blood of Christ, so that to all who partake, with the bread and wine, are at the same time imparted and communicated the real, essential body of Christ, which was given for us, and the blood of Christ which was shed for us.

"The Augsburg Confession, in Art. X, thus expresses it, 'Of the Lord's Supper, we teach that the true body and blood of Christ are really present under the form of bread and wine, and there distributed and received.' *

"This excludes all figurative and substantial presence. We may indeed represent to our minds absent objects as though present, but they are not

* The words "under the form" are not to be understood as meaning that bread and wine do not continue in the Holy Supper but only their "form;" this would be papal transubstantiation; but by the form is meant, the visible parts or elements of the Sacrament, which are unchanged.

really present in their substance; and thus faith can represent the body and blood of Christ as present, but it cannot bring to pass a real presence. It is imaginary and not real. But the body and blood of Christ are present in the Holy Supper in such way, that they are really imparted to us in the bread and wine.

"Things may also be present by their effects and operations, which are not always substantially present at the places where their influence is exerted. For instance, the sun has its influence upon the earth and fills all space with light, which penetrates to the deepest mines; but according to its substance it is not on the earth, but far away in the heavens. The body and blood of Christ are in the Sacrament not only in their effect and influence, but in their substance. But such presence we connect with those visible signs, which according to the words of the institution, indicate that what Christ gives us with the bread to eat is His body and what he gives us with the cup to drink is His blood; and it is not a figurative or spiritual body, but really that body which was given for us and really that blood which was shed for the forgiveness of sins.

"'It is a presence of the whole person of Christ,

of the divine, by its inherent omnipresence, and of
the human through the divine, a presence not
ideal or feigned, but most true; not fleshly, but
spiritual; not after the manner of this earth, but
of the unseen world; not natural, but supernatural.'—(*Krauth*).

"Now, if we are asked, how can these things
be? or to explain the manner and nature of the
presence, our only answer is, that it is divine and
incomprehensible.   We do not see, feel or taste the
body and blood of Christ in the Sacrament, for we
do not parake of them in a carnal or Capernaitish
manner; but we distinguish them from all other
meat and drink, and they are communicated to us
in a manner invisible and unsearchable.   Nor is it
necessary that we should know it or grasp it with
our weak understanding, for it is a mystery and an
article of faith, which we cannot comprehend, but
we are bound to receive it and believe it upon the
highest testimony.*   Hence we believe in a true,

---

* Luther says, "They want to know how Christ's body is in
the bread, and if it cannot be explained to them, they deny its
presence; and yet these same men do not know how to open
their mouths, move their tongues, or grasp a pen in their hands,
and many other smaller things.   I will not say anything about
their not knowing how they see, hear, speak, or live.   All these

substantial presence of the body and blood of Christ, although we do not comprehend the mode, for that is divine and beyond human conception.

"Gerhard, as quoted by Schmid (Hay's and Jacobs' admirable translation, p. 577), says: 'This presence is called Sacramental, because the celestial object in this mystery is bestowed and presented to us through the medium of external sacramental symbols; it is called true and real, to exclude the figment of a figurative, imaginary and representative presence; substantial, to exclude the subterfuge of our opponents concerning the merely efficacious presence of the body and blood of Christ in this mystery; mystical, supernatural and incomprehensible, because in this mystery the body and blood of Christ are present, not in a worldly manner, but in a mystical, supernatural and incomprehensible manner. Some of our theologians have called it a corporeal presence, but only with respect to the object and not at all to the mode; they wish to say by this, that not only the virtue and efficacy, but the substance itself of the body and blood of Christ, is present in the

---

things we constantly feel and yet we do not know how they are brought about, and yet they want to know how Christ's body is in the bread, and will not let Christ be Master."

Holy Supper, for they oppose this word to spiritual presence as it is defined by their opponents,
but by no means wish to say thereby that the body
of Christ is present in a corporeal and quantitative
manner.

"But that others may see what has moved us to
adopt this faith, we must consider the grounds
upon which it is established.

"II. WHAT ARE THE PROOFS OF THE DOCTRINE?

"1. Our first ground for believing this doctrine
is based upon the plain, distinct assurance of our
Lord, 'Take, eat, this is my body,' etc. In these
words, He gives instructions to His disciples concerning a new institution, of which they had as yet
heard nothing, and announces to them its nature
and design.   For without such instruction it would
have appeared very strange to them that, after
partaking of the Paschal lamb and the ordinary
meal, He would offer them a small piece of bread
to eat and the cup from which to take a sip of
wine, as they had already enjoyed both to their
full satisfaction.   Hence He takes bread, gives
thanks, blesses and separates it from a common
use, and gives it to them with the express direction, 'Take, eat, this is my body,' thereby indicat-

ing that something different and more exalted than common bread was given to them, which was His body, and so likewise with the cup.   Now, in order to make the disciples properly understand what He was teaching them, it was necessary for Him to employ plain and distinct words, otherwise they would not have known what they were receiving or what conceptions to entertain respecting it.

"2. We are bound to interpret these words, just as we do other passages of Scripture, according to their plain, natural meaning.   It is a fundamental rule of all Scripture interpretation, not to depart from the real, natural sense of the language without absolute necessity, and when the Scriptures themselves direct us to do so.   For they were not written after any human model or according to human fancy, neither must they be thus expounded, but as the Holy Ghost explains His own meaning through His own words.   Especially must we confine ourselves to the words of the Scripture in the commands and promises of God, the divine mysteries and articles of faith, so that we may not be unawares betrayed into error.   Chemnitz, one of our most eminent theologians, has wisely said: ' The sacraments, because they are mysteries unknown to human reason and concealed from our

senses, and which are made known and revealed
by the Word alone, must therefore necessarily be
interpreted and correctly learned by and according
to the words in which they are announced and delivered to us.' Although figurative language is
sometimes used in the Bible, yet every article of
faith must be expressed in plain, distinct language;
and we have no right to deviate from these natural
words, unless the Scriptures themselves show us
that they were not intended to be understood in a
natural, but in a figurative sense. If we then take
the words of our Lord in their obvious natural
meaning, we cannot understand them in any other
sense than that the body and blood of Christ are
truly present in the Holy Supper. Take and eat,
means, according to the natural understanding of
the phrase, something that is offered and received,
whether by the hand or mouth, and really eaten
and enjoyed as food. That which is offered to the
disciples is called 'this'—this which I give you—
and it is not only bread which they have before
their eyes, but it comprehends the whole thing
which was offered. The little word 'is,' according to the plain, natural understanding of it, does
not mean signifies or represents, but it embraces
that which really exists in it. The word 'body'

means a true, essential body, and not an apparent
body or the sign of a body, and to mark the difference, He says, 'My body,' so that it might not be
understood of the figurative body of the Paschal
lamb, or of any other body.   Hence these words
cannot be understood in any other than the plain,
natural sense, which is this: that which Christ has
ordained in the Holy Supper, and which He gives
us to eat and drink therein, is His true, essential
body and His true, essential blood, given and shed
for the forgiveness of sins.   Every other explanation of the words, involving any change of the elements or regarding them as a bare representation,
is artificial, and is contrary to their natural meaning.

"3. This mode of speech should not seem hard to
adopt or unusual.   When the physician prescribes
a remedy and says, ' Take it; it is a valuable
restorative,' the patient understands the words according to their literal meaning, that in and with
this potion (or whatever it may be) a healing
medicine is offered, and he thinks of no change in
the material or mere sign.   It is a reality.   Our
old writers also illustrate this subject by the dove
which appeared at the baptism of Christ, and by
that other event, his breathing on the disciples.

In Luke iii. 22, we read, 'And the Holy Ghost
descended in a bodily shape like a dove upon
him,' and in John i. 32, 'I saw the Spirit descending from heaven like a dove.' The Holy Ghost
was not changed into a dove, or locally included
therein, but under the form of a dove He was
really present. In John xx. 22, it is said, 'He
breathed on them and saith, Receive ye the Holy
Ghost.' The breath itself was not the Holy Ghost
but only the means through which the Holy Ghost
was communicated to them. Thus in the Holy
Supper, 'Take, eat, this is my body; Take; drink,
this is my blood,' because in, with and under the
eating and drinking of the bread and wine, the
blood and body of Christ are at the same time
communicated to us.

"4. But we must also consider the language as
that of a last will and testament, which should
always be precise and obvious.

"Shortly before His death, our Lord instituted
this memorial of His love, as a testament and be-
quest to His disciples, and sealed it with His blood,
and hence it has all the force and authority of
such a document. In the preparation of a testament, men take special pains to use the most
precise and most intelligible language, so that no

misunderstanding and dissension may ensue;
much more would Christ not employ ambiguous
or obscure words. St. Paul, Gal. iii. 15, says,
'that though it be but a man's covenant, yet if it
be confirmed, no man disannulleth nor addeth
thereto;' this sentiment must apply with greater
force to the last testamentary words of our Lord.
No figurative terms are used in such documents.
The legacy must be described in clear, distinct
words, so that each heir may know what and how
much is his portion of the inheritance. The
division of the property is made agreeably to such
terms, as well as the decision of the executors and
of the courts. Who would be satisfied if he was
distinctly named in a will and a nice farm or a
snug sum of money were bequeathed to him, and
some one would come forward and contend that
the language had quite a different meaning,—that
it was to be understood figuratively, and would try
to deprive him of the legacy itself?—would he not
properly and strenuously insist upon the interpretation of the words as they stand, and not submit
to a perversion of them, to be wheedled out of his
rights? Why should we not allow the testament
of our Lord the same privilege? Why should we
permit the 'abundant riches' which He bequeaths

15

to us in plain words to be wrung from our hands? If others wish to interpret the language differently, they do it at their peril; but they cannot blame us, if to the honor of Christ, we adhere to His simple declaration, and say with Luther, 'My dear Lord Jesus, a terrible dispute has arisen about Thy language in Thy Holy Supper. Some maintain that Thy words are to be understood in a different sense from what they convey. But as these men teach me nothing certain, but only perplex me and raise doubts in my mind, and neither will nor can prove their position, I will stick to Thy text, just as the words speak. If there is anything dark in them, it was Thy will it should be so, for Thou hast given no other explanation of them, nor commanded it to be done.''

"5. The harmony of the Evangelists and of Paul on this subject. The three gospel writers, Matthew, Mark and Luke (John entirely omits the report) use precisely the same words in recording the transaction, 'This is my body,' etc. Now, these inspired men in relating the same events of another character, differ in their language or introduce additional facts connected with the story, and from this we may conclude that the Holy Ghost purposely directed them to use the same

words in relating the fact of the Lord's Supper, so
that we might not in the least degree depart from
their true and obvious meaning. What is more
remarkable, Paul, who wrote a considerable time
after the ascension of our Lord, and who did not
copy his account from the evangelists nor 'receive it from men, but by the revelation of Jesus
Christ,' Gal. i. 12, expressly testifies, that 'I have
received of the Lord, that which also I have
delivered unto you,' and then uses precisely the
same language as the evangelists, 'Take, eat, this
is my body,' etc., etc., and perfectly agrees with
them in all respects. Now, if it had been intended that we should understand the words they
use in a sense different from what they convey, it
is very likely that they would have been so interpreted by Paul, in order to preserve the Church
from error. But he does not teach a doctrine different from that of the gospel writers, but employs
precisely the same words. If, then, a fact is proved
by testimony of two or three witnesses, why should
we not allow the evidence of the three evangelists
and of Paul to prevail, when in this affair they
speak as with one tongue? Our old master, Chemnitz, well says: "He, therefore, who departs from
these repetitions and seeks elsewhere another in-

terpretation, is as ungrateful as contumelious towards the studied accuracy and paternal solicitude
of the Son of God, our preceptor, who alone can
open and expound the closed book."

"In addition to the words of the institution, Paul
describes the Lord's Supper thus, 'The cup of
blessing which we bless, is it not the communion
of (that is, the means of participating in) the blood
of Christ? the bread which we break, is it not the
communion of the body of Christ?' The word
'communion,' as here used, also means communication as it is used in 1 Cor. xi. 17, 18, 21, where
in our English Bible it is called partaking, and in
Heb. xiii. 16, where it is 'communicated,' but it is
the same word in Greek in one or another of its
forms. Thus the bread and wine in the sacrament are such a communion, through which the
body and blood of Christ are really offered and
communicated. If there exists a real communion
between the two objects, so that one communicates
itself to the other, they cannot be separated as the
heavens are from the earth, but there must exist
between themselves a close union. Now Paul says:
'The blessed cup and the blessed bread' are a communion of the body and the blood of Christ, through
which the body and blood of Christ are really com-

municated, and of which we become 'partakers.'
This 'communion' in the sacrament is not spiritual communion or 'fellowship' spoken of in 1 Cor.
i. 9, nor of the benefits of Christ, but of the body
and blood of Christ.   Surely, they must be present
to be 'communicated' to us.   But if all this is to
be understood only as a spiritual communion, it
could not be said that 'the blessed cup and bread'
are the 'communion,' but rather that faith is the
'communion' of the body and blood, because by
faith alone we become partakers of Christ spiritually.   Nor is it to be considered a bare figurative
representation, for the apostle does not say that the
cup and the bread are the signs of the 'communion,' but the 'communion' is the body and blood
of Christ itself.

"6. The truth of our proposition is established
upon the divine character of its blessed Founder.

"It is not without reason that Paul twice declares, 'I have received of the Lord Jesus that
which also I have delivered unto you, that the
Lord Jesus the same night in which he was betrayed took bread,' etc., 1 Cor. xi. 23; xv. 3.
Hence it is the Lord who founded the Supper, and
who has the right to govern all creation, and whom
we are bound to obey; and as this is the Lord, as

the Son of God and God Himself has founded this
ordinance, we dare not mistrust His words nor institutions, but we may be assured that His words
are true. When men commit errors in the use of
language or deceive by their promises, it may be
imputed to their lack of wisdom or their inability
to express themselves correctly, and thus lead to a
misapprehension of their meaning; or it may be
because they are not sincere, and purposely use
ambiguous language; or they may honestly promise and not be able to fulfill their promises; or,
finally, they may intentionally deceive by uttering
that which they know is not true.

"Not one of these imperfections can we impute
to our Lord without blasphemy. His words are
yea and amen. Why then should we not take
Him at His word, and believe what He distinctly
says? One jot of His word is of more value than
all human reason united, and infinitely above a
thousand decrees of Councils.

"7. Our last proof is, the fearful condemnation
which all those bring upon themselves, who unworthily partake of the Lord's Supper.

"Paul describes such as being guilty of the body
and blood of Christ, 1 Cor. ii. 27, 29, eating and
drinking damnation (judgment) to himself, not dis-

cerning the Lord's body. The apostle does not
say, that unworthy partakers render themselves
'guilty' of Christ, nor of His honor, nor of His
ordinance, but expressly of His 'body and blood,'
and that unworthily eating and drinking, which
blame or inculpation, if it has any meaning at all,
must depend upon the presence of the body and
blood, and this offence consists in 'not discerning
the Lord's body.'

"Here we will again quote from Dr. Krauth's
Conservative Reformation, p. 643: 'To discern'
means to 'make or put differences between'—to
distinguish between two things which there is a
liability of confounding—to mark the distinction
between one thing and another. The point of the
apostle is, That which you receive in the Lord's
Supper is not mere bread and wine, as your conduct would imply that it is, but it is also the body
and blood of Christ; therefore your guilt (taking its
root in your failure to discern this body and blood)
is not that of the abuse of the bread and wine, but
of the indignity offered to His body and blood which
they (the bread and wine) communicate; therefore
your punishment is not simply that of men guilty
of gluttony and drunkenness, but that of men
guilty of a wrong done to the body and blood of

Christ; therefore sickness and death have been sent to warn you of your awful crime, and if these warnings be not heeded, your final doom will be to perish with the world.

"Now, if on the other hand, we are to understand this of a merely spiritual partaking, we cannot say of the 'unworthy' that they render themselves 'guilty of the body and blood of Christ,' for they cannot spiritually partake of these because of their unworthiness and unbelief; true, by their unbelief they make themselves 'guilty' of or against Christ; but they cannot sin against the body and blood of Christ, if both are not present. Besides, there is no necessity of 'discerning' the Lord's body, if the unworthy receive nothing in the sacrament but the external bread and wine. If a bare 'representation' of the body and blood of Christ is to be made in the sacrament, it cannot be said that the unworthy can make themselves 'guilty of the body and blood of Christ' in not 'discerning the Lord's body,' but they make themselves guilty only of the external signs thereof, and do not properly 'discern' (or discriminate) such signs from the ordinary partaking of food and drink. But this is not the obvious meaning of the apostle's language, for according to that the essen-

tial presence of the body and blood are necessary
to render this self-inculpation possible. One of
our old theologians (Danhauer) uses this language:
The apostle seems scrupulous in the choice of his
words, and says, 'He is guilty of (that is, he sins
against) not the bread, not the soul of Christ, but
the body and blood of the Lord, just as Judas
sinned against the cheek of the Saviour when he
kissed it with his treacherous lips, just as the mur-
derers of Christ made themselves guilty of the innocent blood which they cruelly shed; just as he
who hears the word of God with his outward ear
but rejects it in his heart, sins against that word.''

CONSECRATION AND ADMINISTRATION.

The sacramental union of the body and blood of
the Lord with the bread and wine takes place at
the moment of the eating and drinking of the
latter. The consecration of the visible elements
is, however, of the greatest importance, for it is the
preliminary step leading up to the ultimate purpose
of the Saviour, to wit, the Sacramental union.
The consecrated bread and cup are set apart from
a common to a divine use, which is in harmony
with the original institution of the Supper, and
which, accordingly, meets the good pleasure of the

Lord. The elements thus dedicated are distributed to each communicant, with the words of the institution and such other Scriptures as are adapted to calling to mind the purport of the Sacrament. Both the consecration and the distribution, in my view, must be done by the regular minister and by no other. Inasmuch as God's promises are yea and amen, this means of grace is valid, irrespective of the moral and spiritual condition of the officiating minister. If he were an angel, nothing would be added, and if he were a devil, naught would be subtracted.

BENEFITS.

Although each communicant participates in the body and blood of the Lord, only those who believe receive the benefits designed to be effected by this Sacrament. All others eat and drink to their condemnation, as Paul says: "He that eateth and drinketh unworthily, eateth and drinketh condemnation to himself, not discerning the Lord's body."

The following are among the chief favors conferred on the worthy and believing communicant. First, the confirmation and sealing of the promise of the remission of sins. I do not say that the observance of this institution secures the forgiveness of sins, for the same was actually granted before, *but it seals and confirms, in a visible manner, that pardon has already been obtained.*   As in the sacrament of baptism we have the assurance that the Holy Ghost is given to regenerate and sanctify, so in the supper one has the guarantee that the body and blood of the Lord is communicated to confirm and ratify the previous work of the Holy Spirit, and the results of his work—Justification, Regeneration, and Sanctification.

Secondly, the communion strengthens faith in Jesus Christ.   The Saviour herein personally imparts himself to the communicant, which implies that He is a living and glorified Lord.   The external elements are truly emblems of his broken body and shed blood—of his death; but they are also, in their very nature, true symbols of life and strength, and thus of His resurrected and immortal life.   Now, the visible sign and the invisible fact —the reception of the living Lord—establish and increase faith in the once crucified, but now living Lord of glory.

Thirdly, another benefit is the augmentation of love to Christ and to man.   This grace is strong or weak in direct ratio to faith.   The latter grasps Christ in all His fulness, and the former follows up with the alabaster box of ointment. Furthermore, in proportion as one loves Christ one also loves all brother men. The question, How can I come into closer sympathy and fellow feeling with "my neighbor?" is readily answered in the light of the above proposition. Live in greater affection and sympathy with Christ, the Creator, and you will live in like manner with man, the creature. *Love to Jesus Christ is the solvent of all questions concerning charitable and missionary operations and enterprises.*

Lastly, the Eucharist is effectual in brightening hope and working joyful gratitude and praise. Faith, love, hope, these three. As one is, so is the other. Although the grace of hope has no place in the world to come, it does have place in this. It is the anchor of the soul, which keeps us sure and steadfast upon the fitful and stormy sea of life. It is the rudder which enables us to sail straight toward the heaven of eternal peace. But in whatever soul these graces find their fullest development and most perfect work, there also is grateful praise and joyful adoration. *The smallest and the largest blessings alike are recognized as the gift of God, and to Him will be ascribed all honor and power and glory for ever and ever.*

LECTURE X.

PRAYER.

1 THESS. v. 17.

1 Thess. v. *17*.   Pray without ceasing.

LECTURE X.

It is just possible that this is not the most suitable place to take up the subject of prayer. Prayer is not a means of grace, but rather a means to grace. Properly speaking, it is not employed by the Lord to restore a sinner to His favor, but it is employed by the repentant sinner for purposes which will be indicated in the progress of this lecture. In view of the character of this exercise it follows, chronologically, the next lecture, Salvation. In order, however, to prevent diversion of attention, and to aid continuity of thought, from Salvation to Glorification, I shall introduce this subject at this point.

I. I call your attention, first of all, to the essential character of prayer. Montgomery sings:

"Prayer is the soul's sincere desire,
  Uttered or unexpressed,
 The motion of a hidden fire
  That trembles in the breast.

(231)

"Prayer is the burden of a sigh,
    The falling of a tear ;
The upward glancing of an eye
    When none but God is near.

" Prayer is the simplest form of speech
    That infant lips can try ;
Prayer the sublimest strains that reach
    The Majesty on high.

"Prayer is the Christian's vital breath,
    The Christian's native air,
His watch-word at the gate of death—
    He enters heaven with prayer."

We are greatly assisted in the discussion of our
subject by calling to mind three facts concerning
God and man. First, God is an infinite being. As
such nothing can be added to His perfections and
plans. He is all-wise, all-powerful, all-merciful
and all-loving. Not a single point of information
can be communicated to Him, not one iota of power
can be added, neither can His moral attributes be
more fully excited and evoked toward His creatures.
This involves the fact that God's providential purposes and plans in behalf of man are perfect and
complete; and inasmuch as God is the same from
eternity to eternity, it follows that these purposes
and plans are now what they have been, and will

always be what they are now. Is not therefore prayer excluded? Certain it is that the creature will not be allowed to break down, by his prayers, the plans of the Creator.

The second fact to be remembered is, that God is most truly a Father to His people. As such He has made abundant provision for prayer. His providential plans are not only comprehensive, but all-comprehensive, including the motions of the soul of man in meditation and prayer. Thus while prayer is not needed to add aught to God's perfections, or to cause Him to alter His plans, it to the contrary absolutely demands those perfections and plans precedent to this act.

By reason of the attributes of omniscience and omnipotence, God was perfectly competent to establish His general providence, at the very beginning, with a view to all the prayers that would ever be made relative to that general providence. In this, as in every other realm, God's foreknowledge preceded, and His foreordination followed. Likewise touching the matter of special or particular providence. He who made us knew from the first what the thoughts, aspirations and prayers of each soul would be, and surely it must have been an easy matter for Him to so arrange

16

all things as to respond to our individual prayers, in the fulness of time, after they are lifted to His ears.

At this juncture the question naturally arises, are there any miraculous answers to prayer? The answer depends on our conception of miracles. If by miracle we hold of an event that it is outside of the original plan of divine movement, or beyond the "reign of law," then I answer in the negative. If on the other hand, our notion of a miracle makes it to be an event simply above, and sometimes contrary to the ordinary course of nature, then I answer in the affirmative. In this view tens of thousands of answers to prayers are miraculous. Allow me to illustrate. I take an extreme case. Suppose a dear friend has died. You have faith to believe that God can restore. You act on that faith, and pray for His restoration to life. God answers your prayer by touching the requisite hidden forces, and your friend lives. This is a miracle, for it is contrary to the ordinary course of things. But note, that this is not a miracle in such sense as to exclude the purpose and plan of God from eternity relative to this very event. In the beginning, when He planned and ordained the existent universe, God knew of this death and prayer. He determined to answer your request. So determining, all the necessary factors entering into that answer were already brought into play, either potentially or absolutely. When the time came to give the answer, it was done; and that as we have already seen, without the slightest violation of the "laws of nature"—concerning which so many scientists are so badly frightened.

It may be profitably remarked here that the answers to many prayers are not accounted miraculous, because they are open and visible. In many cases answers can be returned by the very persons who offer the prayer. It does not follow, however, that these are not direct answers from God; for if He had not taken these prayers into consideration, matters would not have been so arranged as that the answers could come after the manner they do.

The third fact I mention is, that as *God* is not only *Creator*, but also a *Father;* so are *men* not only *creatures*, but also *children.* The relation existing between God and men is, therefore, that of father and children. All the facts and principles involved in every well-ordered earthly family are, accordingly, identical with those in this "family of God." Now, in an earthly family the children ought to possess a spirit of dependence, trust, prayer and

love. They ought to realize their need of the favor
and counsel of their father; they should confide in
his willingness and ability to assist them; and furthermore, they should be encouraged to freely and
fully unbosom their desires and wishes to him.
Surely where these things exist, there will tender
and sincere affection reign supreme. Transfer this
argument to the higher realm, and we at once ap-
prehend the true philosophy of our subject. In this
view, it becomes apparent that prayer becomes absolutely essential in man's relation to his heavenly
Father. Although God's providential plans toward
him were fixed from of old, this does not militate
against the fullest outflow of the soul toward Him.
For I desire to emphasize again, that it was in view
of such prayer that the Father decreed His benign
economy. Every one may be fully persuaded that
his prayers go up before God, to be heard and answered. Let us rejoice that we can "come to a
throne of grace boldly, to obtain grace to help in
time of need." "He that cometh to God must
believe that He is, and that He is a rewarder of
them that diligently seek him." "Ask and ye
shall receive, seek and ye shall find, knock and it
shall be opened unto you." "Whatsoever ye ask
the Father in my name, that will I give unto you."

These promises, with hundreds more of the same import, establish the fact that "the effectual, fervent prayer of the righteous man availeth much." The action and reaction of prayer are alike salutary; the former in evoking God's gifts and blessings upon man, the latter in evoking the noblest parts of man as a gift and offering to God.

What more shall I say relative to the nature and character of prayer? This will I say: It is the meek, childlike, trusting, loving cry of the creature to the infinite Creator, in the sweet assurance of tender audience and cheerful response.

II. I now crave your attention for the consideration of a few characteristics of true prayer.

If I am not mistaken, there prevails a great deal of mist and fog around our subject in the minds of good people. People are frequently perplexed over the many seemingly unanswered prayers they and others have lifted to God. They are at a loss to reconcile the teachings of the Scriptures on this subject with certain indisputable cases of unanswered prayers. Doubtless the fault lies somewhere, that such is the case. Inasmuch as it cannot attach to God, it must attach to man. "Ye pray and receive no answer, because ye pray amiss."

Let us note that all the legitimate objects of prayer are divisible into two classes: Those for which prayer may be made conditionally, and those for which prayer may be offered unconditionally. The objects belonging to the first class are the temporal gifts and blessings; those in the second class are the spiritual favors—that is, all endowments that actually enter into man's growth in grace and in the knowledge of the Lord. In respect to all matters outside of the last named, man must recognize the fact that his desires and will and the will of God may be dissimilar. Man is short-sighted and knows not always what is best for him—his wants are by no means always his needs, and his desires and his truest interests often collide. Hence, if he is a trustful child of God, he will always pray: "Not my will, but Thine be done." This constitutes the condition alluded to. In respect to the spiritual blessings above mentioned, there are no conditions limiting and governing prayer. Petitioning the Father for His grace and the gift of His Spirit, surely must always be in accord with His will and pleasure; and since there is certainty as to that, man's will and God's agree, and hence the prayer ought to be absolute.

Owing to the fact that many people do not dis-

criminate between objects of prayer, they petition
the throne of grace in the same unconditional manner for all blessings whatever. God in His goodness and mercy sees fit to withhold many of
the things asked for. Thereupon those who are
denied what they have urged, become perplexed
and discouraged, and frequently fall into doubt and
despair. But all this time the blame belongs to
them, and not to the Father.

We must make account of another characteristic
belonging to our subject. It is this: there are two
distinct factors inseparably connected with all true
prayer. They are *faith* and *works.* The former
we understand of an implicit reliance and trust in
our God and Saviour. It is a feeling of assurance
that the heavenly Father will verify every promise
on record, in His own way and time. By the latter is meant a thorough co-operation with God in
the direction of the offered prayers. I said at another place that the petitioner may occasionally be
the agent in securing an answer to his supplica-
tions. For instance, one appeals for his "daily
bread." Ordinarily the way to bring the answer
is to employ the strength and talents God supplies,
laboring for it. Another presses his suit in behalf
of the conversion of a friend. Now let him work

toward that end in personal appeal, and especially
in the presentation of the gospel, and the end
designed will likely be speedily realized. These
illustrations suffice to indicate my thought.

I submit that nine-tenths of the unanswered
prayers are due to the lack of one or the other, or
both, of these factors. In this, as in the matter
of salvation, "faith without works is dead," and
works without faith are a mockery. In all religious
acts and movements these two are joined together
by Him who made us, and no man must put them
asunder. Supply these two factors—with all they
necessarily imply—and the question of answers is
solved. All that is agreeable to the will of God
will be unfailingly forthcoming. "Pray as if
all depended on God, and work as if all depended
on yourself"—that puts an end to all speculations.

III. The form of prayer is a matter that challenges our attention briefly.

As a man comes into the presence of God in the
act of prayer, various thoughts pass over the disc of
his mind. In that presence he thinks of the greatness and majesty of Him whom he is about to address. He calls to mind that God is the creator,
preserver and benefactor of all things in the universe; that He is infinite in perfections, and eternal

in existence. These truths recognized will con-
strain one to utter words of adoration. This is
usually the first part of prayer. The Scriptures
furnish us most beautiful and striking expressions
of adoration. The introduction to the Lord's
Prayer is most beautiful on account of its great
simplicity and evident sincerity: "Our Father who
art in heaven." At Acts iv. 24, the apostles introduced their appeal in sore trial thus: "Lord, thou
art God, which hath made heaven and earth and
the sea and all that in them is." Daniel began a
prayer, "O Lord, thou great and awe-inspiring
God, keeping the covenant and mercy to them that
love Him and to them that keep His commandments." Approaching the heavenly Father with
such form of sound words on his lips, the worshiper
fills his mind with a proper spirit of reverence and
devotion.

From Adoration there is a natural and almost
necessary transition to Confession. The soul having dwelt on the character of God in adoration,
will now inevitably turn back to self. What a
contrast! God so exalted, and man so abased. God
so wise and mighty and pure, and man so ignorant
and weak and sinful. God so condescending and
true to man, and man so rebellious and unfaithful

to God.   In the presence of the Lord, man sees the
sinfulness of sin as nowhere else, which may well
cause him to cry out: "What is man that Thou
art mindful of him, or the son of man that Thou
visitest him?"

As one perceives the weakness of his spiritual
strength and the impurity of his holiness, and
remembers that all his sufficiency is from God, how
ready is he to acknowledge the one, that he may
receive the other.   Abraham called himself "dust
and ashes."   Job declares: "Behold, I am vile,
what shall I answer thee?"   David says: "For I
acknowledge my transgression, and my sin is ever
before me.   Against thee, thee only, have I sinned,
and done this evil in thy sight."   Isaiah exclaims:
"Woe is me, for I am undone; because I am a man
of unclean lips, and I dwell in the midst of a people of unclean lips."   Daniel confesses: "We have
sinned, and have committed iniquity, and have
done wickedly, and have rebelled, even by depart-
ing from thy precepts."   The Word is full of con-
fessions similar to the foregoing.   Who but makes
like acknowledgment, as he faithfully draws the
contrast between self and Jehovah?

The step from Confession to Thanksgiving is
short and easy.   Adoration and confession, these

necessarily induce praise and thankfulness. The
worshiper delights to recall all the past mercies
and blessings of God, and to meditate upon them,
both for their own sake as having already been enjoyed, and for the reason that they are inspirers of
faith that their Giver will continue to be gracious
in the future. Indeed, present and past favors are
very potent in encouraging the child of God to make
application for future good. Who, however, is base
enough to recall and ponder upon these things
without an overflow and outflow of grateful praise?
Surely not he who is right before the Lord. Let
us turn again to the Holy Scriptures. In the ninth
Psalm we find these words: "I will praise Thee,
O Lord, with my whole heart; I will show forth all
Thy marvelous works." Again, in the ciii. Psalm:
"Bless the Lord, O my soul, and all that is within
me bless His holy name." In David's prayer,
on the occasion of Solomon's regal association with
him, we find the following sublime utterance:
"Blessed art Thou, Lord God of Israel, our Father,
for ever and ever. Thine, O Lord, is the greatness
and the power and the glory and the victory and
the majesty; for all that is in the heavens and in
the earth is Thine; Thine is the kingdom, O Lord,
and Thou art exalted as head above all. Both

riches and honor came of Thee, and Thou reignest
over all, and in Thy hand is power and might, and
in Thy hand it is to make great and to give strength
to all.   Now, therefore, our God, we thank Thee
and praise Thy glorious name." Jesus once prayed:
"I thank Thee, O Father, Lord of heaven and
earth." Again, "Father, I thank Thee that Thou
hast heard me." Paul writes to the Philippians:
"In everything by prayer and supplication, with
thanksgiving, let your requests be made known
unto God."

The last part that belongs to the form of prayer
is Petition.   This is prayer proper.   In this the
suppliant makes his appeal to Him from whom
cometh "every good and perfect gift," who also is
"the Author and Finisher of our faith."   Inasmuch
as this phase of the subject was sufficiently discussed in the early part of this lecture, nothing
further will be remarked in this place, except to
say that the Old and New Testaments contain unceasing exhortations to prayer.   All through the
Bible men are encouraged to call upon God for all
they need—things great and small; with the assurance that He will hear and answer.

IV. Prayer is the instinct of the regenerate
heart.

The pious in all the ages past have delighted in this exalted and exalting exercise. Dr. Patton writes on this point as follows: Prayer evidently accompanied the accepted sacrifice of Abel, as he stood by his slain lamb, confessed his sin, and implored divine mercy. It must have been the breath of the spiritual life of the holy Enoch, during those three hundred years in which he "walked with God." It was the characteristic of Abraham, "the friend of God," who carried to His divine Friend all thoughts and plans for himself and for those he loved. Isaac and Jacob were praying men; and it was from this fact that the latter gained his immortal name of Israel—Prince of God; because of his urgent prayer he gained a victory as one possessed of power like a prince. Moses had special power in this direction, and prevailed wonderfully in intercession for others. Samuel was noted for the same trait, and when he resigned his judgeship, the people made it their parting request that he would not cease to pray for them. David was always on his knees, if we may judge from his Psalms, which are as much prayers as praises, and in one of which he describes his own habits as follows: "Evening and morning and noon will I pray, and cry aloud, and

He shall hear my voice." His faith in this for all
men, as well as for himself, led him to say: "O
Thou that hearest prayer, unto Thee shall all men
come." Elijah, the petitioner, is as famous as
Elijah, the reprover and reformer; so that in the far
away time of the New Testament Church, he
could be held up as an example and encourage-
ment in prayer, by James, who, in illustration of
his assertion that the effectual fervent prayer of
a righteous man availeth much, said: "Elias was
a man subject to like passions as we are, and he
prayed earnestly that it might not rain, and it
rained not on the earth on the land where he
lived, for a period of three years and six months;
and he prayed again, and the heavens gave rain
and the earth brought forth her fruit." To name
no other Old Testament saint, Daniel will stand
forever associated with a willing martyrdom, so to
speak, on behalf of this duty and privilege, as will
His deliverance ever be a monument of its power.

The New Testament saints kept the same characteristics. One of the earliest personages in the
history is Anna, of whom it is said that "she
departed not from the temple, but served God with
fastings and prayers, day and night." Simeon
was of kindred spirit, as were Zacharias and Eliza-

beth, and Joseph and Mary. Jesus not only taught
His disciples to pray, and Himself offered petitions
publicly, on various recorded occasions, but sometimes spent whole nights in prayer, alone upon the
mountain tops or in the wilderness; and it was
with praying breath that He expired upon the
Cross. The testimony borne concerning thousands of converts made on the day of Pentecost is:
"They continued steadfastly in the apostles' doctrine and fellowship, and in breaking of bread and
in prayers." The apostles themselves prayed for
ten days, steadily, prior to that scene of wonders;
and in every new trial or difficulty which occurred,
we read of their uniting in solemn petition for
aid. Paul, the last and greatest of the apostles,
was full of the spirit of supplication; and not only
does the book of Acts contain references to many
occasions on which he prayed, as for instance, in
the prison at Philippi, and the parting scene at
Miletus, but his epistles constantly allude to the
earnestness and fervency of his prayers for individuals and churches, and abound in commands and
exhortations to Christians to pray in turn for him,
and to maintain the habit of prayer "without
ceasing."

The history of the Church since the apostolic

days has presented the same aspect. Luther, speaking of his use of the Lord's Prayer, says, "For to this day, I suck still at the Pater Noster, like a child; I eat and drink thereof like a full grown man, and can never have enough." It was said of him "that he could have what he would of God." It is related of him by one who heard him on a certain occasion, that his tone was reverent as if speaking to his Maker, and yet he maintained the confidence of one who is conversing with a sympathizing friend. At one time there was a crisis in the affairs of the Reformation. Persecution had broken out. Friends were few and weak, while enemies were many and strong. Human weakness must attach itself to omnipotent power. Luther was not dismayed, for he knew the secret of hidden power. His battle-hymn pointed the source: "Ein feste Burg ist unser Gott."

He wrestled alone with God, till like one of old, he had prevailed. Then he went into the room were his family had assembled, with joyous and exultant heart; and raising his hands, with uplifted eyes, he exclaimed: "We have overcome! We have overcome!" It afterwards proved that just at that time, the Emperor Charles V. issued his proclamation of religious toleration in Germany.

Doubtless Luther had pleaded this Scripture:
"The king's heart is in the hand of the Lord,
as the rivers of water; He turneth it whitherso-
ever He will."

Time fails me to speak of the prayers of Me-
lanchthon, Calvin, Zwinglius, and scores of others
since their time, who were mighty with God in
prayer. *"Piety and prayer are synonymus."*

Space forbids that I should recite some of the
endless number of answers to prayer. It is enough
to say that no sooner can God refuse to respond to
His children's cries than that He can deny His
Fatherly nature and character.

The history of MAN *is the history of* PRAYER; *the
history of* GOD *is the history of* ANSWERS *to prayer.*

"Come to the morning prayer;
Come, let us kneel and pray;
Prayer is the Christian pilgrim's staff,
To walk with God all day.

"At noon, beneath the Rock
Of Ages, rest and pray;
Sweet is that shelter from the heat,
When the sun smites by day.

"At evening shut thy door;
Round the home-altar pray;
And, finding there the house of God,
At Heaven's gate close the day,

"When midnight veils our eyes,
  O, it is sweet to say,
I sleep, but my heart waketh, Lord,
  With thee to watch and pray,"

JAMES MONTGOMERY.

LECTURE XI.

SALVATION.

EPH. ii. 8.

Eph. ii. *8.* For by grace are ye saved through faith, and that not of yourselves, but it is the gift of God.

LECTURE XI.

WE now enter upon a subject which of all that have been treated, is the most pleasing and inspiring. Well nigh all which has been said in these addresses leads up to and clusters around this central thought. Every movement of God earthward, from the first promise of a Redeemer to Adam and Eve till the outpouring of the Holy Ghost on the day of Pentecost, had reference, more or less direct, to man's spiritual recovery.

The three specific subjects which enter into our discussion are: Justification, Regeneration and Sanctification. Regeneration and Sanctification are the final ends towards which everything points and moves, as Justification is the immediate end. The Forensic act of God is in order to the Therapeutic. The former is objective to man, the latter subjective.

For the purpose of clearing the way for an intelligent discussion of the matter in hand, I recur briefly to a point or two advanced in the second lecture—"The Fall." You recall that I mentioned that the principal result of the Fall was the disturbance and perversion of man's rational, or spiritual, constitution. This was "Death." This was the infliction of the violated penalty. This was subjective. You also remember that I said there was another result, to wit, the objective—in the mind of God. It was not only proper and right in the Creator to give a just and wise law to the creature, but such was an absolute necessity. The sanction of the law was an exact exponent of the mind of the Law-giver in reference to disobedience. Now, when transgression ensued the penalty must be inflicted, or the Lawgiver's veracity and holiness and all his other moral attributes, will be impeached. This is the only alternative. But the latter is out of the question, and, therefore, the former must be accomplished.

Note well that the voluntary disobedience of the original pair necessarily affected the mind of God concerning them. It did not affect the thoughts of God, as to whether man is a good creature; nor His moral feelings, as goodness, love, etc.; nor yet His will, as touching their salvation. But their transgression did affect Him in such sense as to change His relation to them. Hence we say, for want of better terms, that God became "offended," or "angry" or "alienated;" and that to the end of man's salvation God must be "appeased" and "reconciled." Now, I am not acquainted with any words that could safely be substituted for those above; and hence, although not expressing the precise facts in the case, they should be allowed to stand in theological literature.

I have observed that after the transgression God's relation or position was changed toward the offenders. The penalty of death was laid upon His own dear creatures, made in his likeness and image. This "death," bear in mind, was not only spiritual, but also necessarily eternal. God's word is gone out of His mouth pronouncing this sad truth. Accordingly, this word stands between Him and His children. In this lies His change of relation to them. This removes God from man, because man first removed himself from God. Hence we use the terms mentioned a short time ago.

But God's feelings and purposes for man are not changed. Having loved them from the beginning, He loves them still. He had no pleasure in the death of the sinner, but rather that he should live. Now, in order to save man from *eternal* death, He must deliver him from *spiritual* death; and to accomplish both, God fixed on the plan of Salvation through His Son, as elucidated in Lectures IV and V.

JUSTIFICATION.

The term Justification is interchangeable with "pardon" and "remission of sins." It describes a condition opposite to guilt or condemnation. It is to stand free from charge or indictment. In a court of justice a man can be justified on the ground of innocence and on that of compensation. When it is clearly proved that the arraigned person is not guilty of the matter charged against him, the court acquits him, and he stands justified before the world. Again, on the other hand, if the person were found guilty, and sentence were passed upon him, if he pays the full penalty of the law which he violated, he is justified, also, in the eyes of the civil tribunal, on the ground of compensation.

Now in the matter of man's standing before God, he must himself confess his guilt. By reference to the record at Gen. iii. 8–13, we learn of the trial and confession of Adam and Eve. The same all men have acknowledged ever since. Hence there can be no justification before God, on the ground of innocence. On the ground of compensation there can be none, for that means eternal death, the sentence which the Judge passed upon man, which is the penalty of the violated law.

It is most evident, accordingly, that if man can be at all justified, it must be by a plan devised by the Lawgiver and Judge, and not by any personal merit or compensation. Such a plan is not only contemplated, but already executed. "God so loved the world that He gave His only begotten Son, that whosoever believeth on Him should not perish but have everlasting life." What I believe to be the true philosophy of the fact of guilt and the scheme of redemption, leads me to so say that the matter of which man needs pardon or justification is eternal death. It is this, as I said sometime ago, that stands between God and the sinner, and which constitutes God's change of relation to, or alienation from man. I then said that God's word had gone forth and must stand, except in the event of a plan by which He is justified—that is, vindicated—to recall it. Just so soon as the word or sentence is nullified, so soon will God be changed again to his former attitude and relation to man; and just so soon God will draw nigh to man, to help him to overcome the subjective result of his disobedience. In the plan of salvation, Jesus Christ takes man's place, and in his stead suffers an adequate amount to justify God in recalling the sentence of death. The blood of the Lamb is sufficient to vindicate God's veracity, justice and holiness, and to show forth at the same time the greatness of His love and tender mercy.

I am now ready to announce a principle, for which nearly all that I have remarked in this address has been preparatory. It is this: *The work and merits of the God-man, the Saviour, being placed to man's credit, God justifies all mankind, everywhere, once for all.*

Please observe that this pardon is a free and full preliminary forensic act, which restores man to the same legal relation to God that he enjoyed before the Fall. It simply negatives the objective consequence of the transgression, but not the subjective. It is in the realm of the legal, and not of the moral, relation of man to God. But it involves the fact that God will now undertake to change man's moral relation to Him, also. In fact, as you see, the legal aspect is precedent to the moral, and altogether in the interest of the latter.

Hence, in view of this universal pardon and justification, God bestows the Holy Spirit upon absolutely every soul which comes into existence.

God makes a sincere and earnest effort to deliver every man from the fact of eternal and, therefore, spiritual death; and although this is effected in only comparatively few cases, the blame attaches to man and not to God.

These statements I make with a full knowledge of the fact that they will be resisted by some who hear them; but such things cannot deter me from averring what I am fully persuaded is in accord with the spirit of the Bible and "a sound mind."

There is, however, another matter to claim our attention at this juncture. It is the subject of *Justification by Faith.*

How can a sinner be just before God? Not by works of righteousness which he can do, but by faith in Jesus Christ. In the universal justification discussed above, voluntary action is not considered. In spite of all the influence of God to the contrary, man has it in his power, as a matter of course, to voluntarily violate the laws of his Maker. In point of fact, this is exactly what most men do.

The Faith, accordingly, which is involved in a sinner's pardon, must not be regarded in the nature of an instrument, or even condition, to such pardon; but the rather as the faculty or eye by which that pardon is apprehended. The only agent en-

tering into the obtainment of the person's justification is Jesus Christ; but faith sees and appropriates
that justification.   Faith must, in view of the
foregoing, have credit as a seeing and appropriating
eye and hand; and it is clearly evident that without this a man cannot enjoy the peace of forgiveness, nor can his life and conduct be such as is
characteristic of the justified soul; for he will not
co-operate with God in his spiritual restoration
like one who realizes his justification.   In my view
every demand of Scripture touching justification by
faith is fully met in the foregoing proposition, and
here I discontinue this subject.

REGENERATION.

This, surely, is a most vital subject.   It is of un-
dying interest, and claims our faithful attention in
its treatment.   "Verily I say unto you, ye must be
born again."

Theologians state the nature and character of
this doctrine in such terms as these: "It is the in-
working or exciting of faith by the Holy Ghost
through the means of grace."   "It is the deposit-
ing of a principle or germ of righteousness."   "It is
the conferring, by the Spirit, of a new heart, feelings and affections."   Such definitions, in the na-

ture of the case, cannot be very wide of the mark. Indeed, I believe them to be harmless, but the trouble is that they afford no great amount of information for those who hunger and thirst after knowledge.

A very fascinating and plausible scientific explanation of this doctrine is ventured by Prof. Drummond, in his very suggestive volume entitled: "Natural Law in the Spiritual World." The position of the book is that the laws in the physical world are identical with those which prevail in the spiritual world. In the chapter relating to the subject now in hand, his argument is about as follows: In the physical world there are three distinct kingdoms, the mineral, the vegetable, and the animal. Now, neither of the lower kingdoms can pass to the next higher. There is a great gulf fixed between each of these realms, and it is never in the power of the lower to lift itself to any place above itself. It is competent, however, for the organic to reach down to the inorganic, and imparting to it organic life, bring it up into the organic kingdom. So, also, does the animal kingdom reach down to the vegetable to lift it up to a place with itself. We notice here that the higher is always the active and all-sufficient agent, and the lower is entirely passive. The argument is constructed on the accepted fact that life comes from life and is never spontaneous. This I wholly accept, so far. This Prof. Drummond now proceeds to apply to the matter of the new birth. Upon his theory of the identity of law in the natural and spiritual worlds, he has easy work to show that man is dead in reference to spiritual life, as the inorganic is dead to organic, and organic to animal life. Accordingly, the spiritual world must reach down to man, and, endowing him with spiritual life, raise him into relation with itself. He affirms that the life in this case is Christ. The whole argument is, to say the least, very captivating. The present speaker cannot, however, give his adhesion to it, for the reason following: I do not agree (if I may venture to disagree with such a profound scholar) to the Professor's position relative to the identity of "laws" in the two spheres indicated. The point of disagreement lies in this: The Professor seems to believe, and I do not, that man, in his sphere, is dead, in the same sense that the various kingdoms in the natural world are in theirs. This reduces man to the level of a natural mechanism. Of course, there is a sense in which such a position may be defended; but it is a sense which requires that man be contemplated from the lowest point of view. In the lecture—"The Creation of Man"—it was shown that man is a great deal more than a lump of flesh; that he is also spirit; that, consequently, he partakes of the very nature of God. The Fall, most assuredly, marred his spiritual visage, but that does not involve the destruction of his spiritual nature. This he still retains, for that is the realm of the soul. Hence, Prof. Drummond's theory that man is dead, in the same sense as nature is dead, and that he must be endowed with a germ of life, so to speak, in order that he may become a spiritual being, and all in spite of man's passivity and natural deadness, I for one do not believe. This I believe to be contrary to right interpretation of Scripture, and to a true psychology, and to personal experience; for all these, with one voice, declare that a man has some share in his "birth from above." After raising this dissentient note, I feel to say that the argument of Dr. Drummond in question is most beautiful and potent, as showing the *analogy* between God's working in nature and in grace. As the mineral never can come up into the vegetable, and the vegetable into the animal, except as the higher forces reach down and bring them up, so it

is precisely true that man cannot attain to the new
birth, except as God supplies needed grace.   In
this lies the analogy.   But man can, and the afore-
said kingdoms cannot, co-operate with the grace
that affects him.   Herein breaks down the alleged
identity.

In this connection I wish to say that what I
have so far said applies mainly to those who are
capable of voluntary action—that is, to adults
rather than to children.   Of this I shall speak
more fully presently.

It now remains for me to advance what I regard
as the philosophy of the doctrine of Regeneration.
This will not occupy much time.   If the Fall en-
tailed death, then I hold that regeneration restores
life.   In the second lecture,—"The Fall"—I ventured to advance what I hold concerning spiritual
death.   It is this: The "spirit" in man was
appointed to rule over the whole man, and the
"flesh" was destined to be subject to, and servant
of, the "spirit."   Spiritual death consists in the
reversal of this order, and so the "flesh" is now on
the throne.   It follows that all the powers and faculties of the soul have become blunted and weak-
ened, and therefore disabled to fulfill their high
and holy functions.   This involves the further fact

of man's alienation from his Maker (God), and his enmity to the will of God. (See last division ot Lecture II.)

From the foregoing it is easy to see that regeneration is the restoration of man. Right here I take the opportunity to say that I refuse to believe that the new birth implies the conferment on man of a principle or germ of life, precisely as this is the case in the natural world. I believe that God's working in regeneration is to rehabilitate the "spirit" of man, and that not contrary, but according, to the laws of the mind. The process must be after this fashion: The Intellect must be enlightened, the Rational Susceptibility must be excited, and the Will must be quickened. This done, all is done—in the way of regeneration. The "spirit" has now assumed its proper place, and functions, and prerogative, and the man is now ready to "keep the body under," henceforth.

The agents by which regeneration is effected are the Holy Spirit and the Scriptures; and in the case of those who do not have access to the Scriptures, tradition and the light of nature. Truth is requisite to bring about all that was mentioned touching the Intellect, Emotions and Will; but this truth, of course, must be of a character adapted to

18

the nature of the work it is to accomplish, and it
must be energized and applied by the Holy Ghost.
Allow me to illustrate my meaning of the foregoing
discussion : Suppose a wicked man on a certain
Sunday morning, contrary to his habit, attends
divine worship. He takes a pew in the rear of
the church, and, as a matter of course, is listless
and uninterested. The minister announces his
text, and the sermon is delivered. The man in
the pew was struck when the text was announced,
and during the progress of the sermon the following has taken place in swift succession: The first
arrest of attention was succeeded by a breaking in
of light, or knowledge, in respect of self and of
God, such as he never had before. This knowledge
is followed by a quickening of emotions running
exactly in the same direction as his knowledge,
and this knowledge and these feelings, according
to mental laws, influence the Will. An alternative is presented to the Will, in form something
like this: "I *know*, I *feel* my relation and duty to
God, and His just claims upon me. Shall I for-
swear my past life and enter upon a life of purity
and obedience, or no?" So far the Holy Spirit
and the Word have done the work, except that the
man has voluntarily opened himself to their in-

fluences. But at this point the man must co-operate with the objective forces, if he desires to be born from above. I assume that he says, "I yield." This is the supreme moment of his life, for he is now restored to "life." He is a "new creature in Christ Jesus; old things have passed away, behold all things have become new."* In this choice of the "better part," there is a radical change of the spiritual disposition, *and that is Regeneration.*

I desire to say here that all this which I assume to take place in the space of a preaching service of say one hour, may as easily transpire in five minutes; and on the other hand, it may occupy days, and even years. The precise time of regeneration, proper, is at the yielding of the will, which necessarily can be but a moment, but the steps leading thereto occupy a shorter or longer time.

I have to say yet that it is at this moment that, life coming into the dead, the "new creature" in Christ enters into loyal and obedient relation with his God and Saviour. God is not only reconciled to him, but he is also reconciled to God, which gives him the spirit of adoption, and he is enabled to say, "Abba Father," and the love of God is shed abroad in his heart by the Holy Ghost which was given unto him.

Now before I leave this subject, I am anxious to say something more in regard to the relation of this doctrine to children.

I repeat here what I intimated once before, to wit, that my remarks thus far have special reference to such as are capable of voluntary action. In the address on baptism I observed that there is a radical difference between the "death" of children and that of wicked adults. The "death" of the latter is deepened and intensified by voluntary transgression. His moral renovation I described above. In the case of infants there is nothing to hinder us in believing that God may, by His Spirit, in baptism, so affect them in the way of energizing their spiritual nature that in popular language it may be called regeneration, although technically it is not such. I do not think that regeneration, in the truest sense, takes place till the very first voluntary yielding of the child to Christ. That may be at a very early period of life. I myself do not take umbrage at the phrase, "Baptismal Regeneration," although I confess to a mental reservation touching its import.

SANCTIFICATION.

Although in Regeneration man is restored to spiritual life, two results of the Fall remain. One is *physical*, and has reference to the *maladies and death of the body;* the other is *moral*, and has reference to *moral character and action.*

The question is not, could God also have overcome these evils? but the rather, why did God not overcome and banish them? The first question carries with it its own answer. The second question may, or may not, be answerable. I venture, however, this answer: God, in His wisdom, saw fit to allow these strong evidences of the Fall to remain, as showing all men the wrecking power of sin, that so, having these things before their eyes, they may the more implicitly rely on the power of God to keep them from more awful and lasting consequences, even eternal perdition.

It is in place to say here that even these evils are devoid of terror to the Christian. The strength of the physical evil is broken by the plan of Redemption, and the power of the moral evil is exhausted by the divine work of Sanctification. The moral evil in question is a continued trend and bias to wrong, after regeneration. At another place I observed that man's spiritual nature, once dethroned, will be likely to continue for a long time after its re-enthronement to be feeble and void of proper self-assertion. The inferior nature, once occupying the ruling place in man, will likely long clamor, after its impeachment, to reoccupy its former place. Thus there is, as St. Paul declares, a constant warfare between these two. When a man with his mind will serve the Lord, there is a law in his members which wars against the law of his mind. On this account all the regenerate confess the fact of many slips and foibles, and even outright sins.

From these things the Christian is delivered more and more by the Holy Ghost and the means of grace. By these a twofold work is accomplished. There is on the one hand the subduing of the "flesh," and on the other hand the uplifting and strengthening of the "spirit." Thus we are exhorted to put off the old man and to put on the new man, Christ Jesus; also to grow in grace and in the knowledgeof the Lord.

The open secret of the process of sanctification lies in the subject's entire yielding of himself to the agents effecting it. Over-concern about this work in the heart on the part of any one, even to the extent of tearing the hair and rending of garments, will not avail; but a hearty co-operation with the Holy Spirit in the way of holding one's self under His cleansing and invigorating influence is all that is required. For as God has begun a good work within man, so will He also finish it. It is proper that one should daily confess and deplore his spiritual weakness, and lay aside every weight and the sin which doth so easily beset him; but above all he must look to Jesus Christ, the author and finisher of his faith, who is our "wisdom, righteousness, sanctification and redemption."

LECTURE XII.

GLORIFICATION.

MATT. xxv. 34.

Matt. xxv. *34.* Come, ye blessed of my Father, inherit the kingdom prepared for you from the foundation of the world.

LECTURE XII. •

'ELEVEN subjects have been discussed. We now enter together upon the twelfth and last. As our Saviour at, Cana, kept the good wine till the last, so also is it with the subject now in hand. It is the best, and follows all the others.

I believe that man was originally intended for a higher and nobler place and state than Eden and Edenic life. Adam and Eve might have said: "It doth not yet appear what we shall be," but with the feeling of assurance that in some way and at some time there would be a spiritualizing of the flesh and an uplifting of their being into a still more exalted realm of existence. What was contemplated for man in the beginning is, notwithstanding his lapse into sin, made possible in Redemption. Man is again placed in a position that he may be glorified at the right hand of the Majesty on high. In the subjects and doctrines previously treated, it has been shown how this can be the case.

The transition from this world to the next is

characterized by an event with which we are all
familiar. It is death, or rather, "falling asleep."

In the Fall, the seed of bodily death was deposited in man's physical nature. In Redemption,
that seed, in the wisdom of God, and for our discipline, was not dislodged. Through the Fall, death
had a terrible sting. Through Redemption, the
sting of death is extracted, so that the giving up
the ghost is no longer death, but sleep. "Oh
death, where is thy sting? Oh grave, where is thy
victory!" "Death is swallowed up in victory."

DEATH.

"Bodily death," says Dr. J. H. Wythe, "occurs
when the cause of life is removed. Life is not
synonymous with spirit, but is peculiar spiritual
influence on matter, the result of the union of created spirits and elemental matter. When the spiritual essence ceases to act upon the matter of the
organism we say the body is dead, and the disinte-
gration and chemical decomposition succeed."

Prof. Draper writes: "The system of animal life
dies before that of the organic. Of the former the
sensory functions fail first, voluntary motion next,
and the power of muscular contraction, under great
stimulus, still feebly continues. The blood, in

gradual death, first ceases to reach the extremities, its pulsation becoming less and less energetic, so that, failing to gain the periphery, it passes but a little way from the heart; the feet and hands becoming cold as the circulating fluid leaves them, the decline of temperature gradually invading the interior. Some of the organic functions often continue for a time, particularly the secretion and the development of heat."

"With the exception of falling asleep, nothing is so similar to the passing away in death as the sinking of a person into a swoon; yet he who faints experiences little or no suffering before unconsciousness ensues. Perhaps, if artificial stimulants were not applied to restore to his nervous system the power of serving the soul, he would pass from the swoon into death without any further sensation. Such, also, is the condition of all those who, reduced to unconsciousness by excessive cold, are eventually restored to life. Their limbs are benumbed, their blood flows slower and slower, and finally the body stiffens as in death. The only sensation they experience is unconquerable drowsiness and desire to lie down and rest; and though they may be perfectly conscious that sleep may end in death, they nevertheless brave it that they may enjoy the delight of sleep. It is thus established that at the moment of dissolution it has in it nothing that is terrible, that very few persons are clearly conscious of it, and that it is the imagination of survivors that invests it with horrors."— *Zschokke.*

"No case is remembered where persons have returned to life after they were believed to have been dead, that the testimony has not been given to the effect that in the very act of departure the last remembered sensations were not merely pleasurable, but exquisite." A titled lady exclaimed, "Why did you bring me back to earth?" A drowned man passed away with strains of the most delightful music striking upon his ears. The man cut down from the gallows had a vision of entering Paradise, surrounded with all its glories. Now a lady struck dead by lightning, as was supposed, says, "I feel quite sure that death by lightning must be absolutely painless, for I had a feeling of gently dying, dying away into darkness." Surely we do ourselves great wrong, and the Merciful One who made death, also, to cherish the idea that it is dreadful, for a correct and substantiated physiology has demonstrated that in the hour and article of death from disease, for several minutes, and sometimes for hours before departure, the feeling of pain is an absolute impossibility: there may be an appearance of it, but it is a manifest, unfelt muscular disturbance."—*W. W. Hall, M. D.*

"The darkness of death is like the evening twilight, it makes all objects more lovely to the dying."—*Richter.*

I have made these quotations from others rather than to cite at length anything that has come under my personal knowledge. However, by way of substantiating what has been quoted above, I cannot forbear to merely mention in this place the happy experience of a near relative. Tortured with extreme pain for a fortnight, a brief period before death there was total cessation of it. Ecstatic delight filled his whole being, and his departure was unspeakably more enjoyed than the passage from wakefulness to sleep, after a long day of exhausting labor.

In view of all that has been said, I am fully persuaded that the pain and terror of death lies in the knowledge of the fact that after death is the Judgment. Accordingly, all who "die in the Lord," to them there is no "fear in death," nor any physical pain. "For so He giveth His beloved sleep."

THE INTERMEDIATE STATE.

This is a matter touching which no man may dogmatize. God has not seen fit to give us a clear and unmistakable revelation concerning the state and place between death and the resurrection, and hence the few words that I have to offer on this subject are not expected to terminate all future discussion.

My study of the Scriptures leads me to the con-clusion that there is an intermediate place and state. This conclusion is based on the meaning and use of the terms Sheol in the Old, and Hades in the New, Testament. These terms I believe to be synonymous, and expressing the fact of a place in the other world, distinct from Heaven and Hell. I freely admit that there are many who do not read the same meaning from these words that I do, but I feel personally assured of the soundness of this interpretation, which, if. the scope of this lecture permitted, I might fortify by a number of "infal-lible proofs" drawn directly from Holy Writ.

I give it as my opinion that Hades is divided into two parts, one of which is the place of abode of the righteous and the other the prison of the wicked, up to the day of judgment.

On that great day the righteous, in union of

soul and body, will enter upon the full and ineffable fruition of Heaven; as the wicked, in union of soul and body, will be cast into Hell.

I may say here that in addition to the teaching of the inspired word, two independent arguments support the above view. First, an argument derived from the character of the joys of Heaven and the suffering of Hell. Apart from the consideration of what are called the positive rewards and punishments in Heaven and Hell, respectively, a great part, perhaps the major part, of both the former and the latter, are natural—that is to say, they are naturally and inevitably consequential of the moral character of the inhabitants of the respective places mentioned. In other words, the conscience is a very great factor in the bliss of Heaven and the woes of Hell. But conscience necessarily depends on knowledge for the full assertion of itself, either in the direction of peace and joy, or the opposite. Now this knowledge is not only of present moral character, but also includes, pre-eminently, the moral status and personal influence of each during his entire earthly life. This is not all. Inasmuch as moral character and voluntary actions in one's life-time start a train of influences which roll on and on while time lasts, it is obvious that

19

no man can know the complete results of his
earthly career, for good or for evil, until everything
will be revealed in the records of the judgment-day.
Then, and then only, can a man know all the results of all the deeds done in the body. Then,
and then only, will the conscience determine, sub-
jectively, the peace and joy of Heaven; the woe
and terror of Hell. Hence, in the light of the
above, the judgment-day is a necessity, and equally
so is the Intermediate State.

Against this it may be said: "When the soul is
freed from the body, at death, it may at once see
the whole outcome of the influences started in this
life; it may be able to anticipate the future, so that
the past and the future are alike known." To
this I have to say, No, I think not. We have
every reason to believe that the mental activities
and laws of thought are substantially the same in
the spirit world as in this. At least it is quite
certain that no new faculties are superadded to
those which man now possesses. Accordingly, the
future cannot be anticipated or known there any
more than here, for this would imply, in my view,
a species of omniscience; and this of course must
be ruled out of the argument.

Another may say: "But does not God know all

things, both past and future? and will He not reveal the future to every one immediately after death?" To this I have to answer as I did above: No, I think not. Such revelation implies a miracle, which I believe to be an act confined entirely to this world. I say this because I cannot conceive that miracles can serve any good purpose in the Unseen World. I hold, therefore, that God will not likely interfere in the manner intimated by the supposed questioner, which leaves the original argument intact and secure, viz., the fact of an Intermediate State.

Another reason favoring an Intermediate State between death and the resurrection is found in the fact of the separation of soul and body during the interval. My view of the nature and faculties of the soul fits it fully for independent existence, if that were God's will. But that is not His will, for ·He reveals to us His purpose to re-unite soul and body at the end of the world. It is not a question of the soul's capability of independent existence, but rather as to a beautiful propriety, that the re-union of soul and body is ordained of God. Note this: Every good deed on the one hand, as every evil deed on the other hand, is accomplished and committed by the united activity of soul and body,

the soul being the principal and the body the
agent. Surely, therefore, I can see poetic propriety in the resurrection and re-union of the body
with the soul, in order to share, with the latter,
the retributions of eternity.

From this it seems obvious, that the soul does
not immediately after death enter upon the last
stage of existence, but only on an *intermediate or
middle stage*, as in this life on the *first*, and after
the Resurrection and Judgment on the *last and the
best*.

I may further say that I hold to the following
tenets:

1. The wicked in the Intermediate State experience substantially the same pain and anguish as
they will in Hell—only less in degree.

2. The righteous experience substantially the
peace and joy and rest that they will in Heaven—
only less in degree.

3. The righteous develops greatly in every capacity of their nature during this interval.

4. All infants and children are here developed
and trained for citizenship in heaven.

5. All the heathen who live and die without a
knowledge of Christ and the doctrines of salvation,
but who are disposed to live up to the light which

they enjoy, and who would accept Christ in this life if they had opportunity, are in the Intermediate State brought into contact with Christ, and are made meet for the enjoyment and service of heaven.

6. All who were incorrigible in this life, whether enlightened or unenlightened, have in the Intermediate State no "second probation."

HEAVEN.

The second advent of Christ, the Judgment and the end of the world, are three thrilling and awful events. At that day a voice may be heard saying: "Time was, time is, but time shall be no more." Time is swallowed up in eternity: Eternal Hell, and Eternal Heaven. "Depart from me, ye cursed, into everlasting fire, prepared for the devil and his angels." "Come, ye blessed of my Father, inherit the kingdom prepared for you from the foundation of the world."

The two great questions that obtrude themselves constantly in regard to heaven are, "Do we know each other there?" and, "What is the nature and character of the place?" On these two questions allow me to voice my sentiments fully and most eloquently by means of a "string of pearls," selected here and there. This done, my aim and purpose in these addresses will be compassed, *and I will bid adieu, with the fond hope that some good, at least, will be realized out of my humble effort.*

RECOGNITION IN HEAVEN.

"Paul before the throne is and inevitably must be the identical Paul who preached at Athens and was martyred at Rome. When he longed to 'depart and be with Christ' he expected not to be somebody else, but the same individual. Moses died fifteen centuries before the advent of Jesus Christ. Yet there was a personality still existing, who appeared at the time of Christ's transfiguration on the mount, and who was addressed by him as Moses. The prophet Elijah, who had died seven hundred years before was there also. When the great Apostle speaks of his Thessalonian converts as his 'glory and joy in the presence of the Lord Jesus Christ,' he assuredly expected to meet the same persons in heaven that he labored with in Thessalonica. If they were not the same people, and if he could not meet them there, how could they be to him a 'crown' or a 'joy.' This point is clearly in accordance with common sense. Whatever change may be produced by death, personal identity will not be altered by one jot or tittle. The sinner who

sins here will be the same sinner who will be punished in a world of woe. The believer who will
be welcomed by the glad salute, 'Come thou
blessed of my Father,' will be the same person
who on earth had done the Father's bidding.
Without this preservation of perfect identity, the
whole idea of a future retribution of rewards and
punishments would be an absurd impossibility.

"If identity is preserved in eternity, will the faculty of memory also survive the grave? Undoubtedly it will. The obliteration of memory would
amount to a partial destruction of the individual.
It would remove some of Heaven's richest enjoy-
ments. If I cannot remember what my Redeemer
has done and suffered for me, how can I join in the
ever 'new song' of grateful praise before His
throne? The obliteration of memory would take
away the severest and bitterest of sin's just retribution in Hell. Upon this point the description
of Lazarus and the selfish rich man 'in torment'
throws a distinct light, for Abraham said, 'Son,
remember that thou in thy life-time receivedst thy
good things.'

" Put together these two facts (1) personal identity is not lost in eternity, (2) memory remains also
unimpaired. It follows inevitably that we shall

know each other in Heaven. When David cried out over his dead boy, 'I shall go to him, but he shall not return to me,' that bereaved father expected to meet again the child whose spirit had flown to God. Certainly we shall not be more stupid in Heaven than we are on earth. Martin Luther, in his 'Table Talk,' makes much of this intercourse with father and mother and kindred in the heavenly home. Sharp, unpoetic old Dr. Emmons used to say: 'I hope to have some talks with the Apostle in Heaven.'

"That infants will be doomed to the everlasting weakness and helplessness and ignorance of infancy seems to my mind impossible. No mother would ever want to see her darling babe stunted to an unchanged babyhood, even here. It would become a pitiable monstrosity. Half the charm of childhood is its constant growth—its delightful openings like the rose-bud, to new thought and development. The idea of an undeveloped infancy in Heaven would be almost a libel on the Creator! My darling boy will be none the less my own child in the 'Father's house,' because he has increased in stature and knowledge, and in favor with God and man. That I shall know him there I have no more doubt of than I have of the exist-

ence of a heavenly rest. Good Dean Alford struck
a chord in every Christian heart when he sang:

> " 'Oh ! then what raptured greetings
> On heaven's happy shore ;
> What knitting severed friendships up,
> Where partings are no more !' "
> —*Theodore L. Cuyler, D.ˇD.*

A great divine says: "When I was a boy I
thought of heaven as a great shining city, with vast
walls, and domes, and spires, and with nobody in it
except white angels, who were strangers to me.
By and by my little brother died, and I thought of
a great city, with walls, and domes, and spires, and
a flock of cold unknown angels, and one little fellow that I was acquainted with. He was the only
one I knew in it at that time. Then another
brother died, and there were two that I knew.
Then my acquaintances began to die, and the flock
continually grew. But it was not until I had sent
one of my little children to his Grandparent—God
—that I began to think I had got a little in myself.
A second event, a third event, a fourth event, and
by that time I had so many acquaintances in
Heaven that I did not see any more walls, and
domes, and spires. I began to think of the resi-
dents of the Celestial City. And now there have so

many of my acquaintances gone there that it sometimes seems to me that I know more in Heaven
than I do on earth.''

"Many in the other galleries we have heard of,
but these we knew.   Oh, how familiar their faces;
they sat at our tables, and we walked to the house
of God in company.   Have they forgotten us?
Those fathers and mothers started us on the road
of life.   Are they careless as to what becomes of
us?   And these children, do they look with stolid
indifference as to whether we lose or win this battle
for eternity?   Nay; I see that child running its
hand over your brow and saying, 'Father, do not
fret; mother, do not worry.'   They remember the
day they left us.   They remember the agony of the
last farewell.   Though years in Heaven, they remember our faces.   They remember our sorrows.
They speak our names.   They watch this fight for
Heaven.   Nay; I see them rise up and lean over
and wave before us their recognition and encour-
agement.   That gallery is not full.   They are
keeping places for us.   After we have slain the lion
they expect the King to call us, saying: 'Come up
higher.'   Between the hot struggles in the arena
I wipe the sweat from my brow, and stand on tip-
toe, reaching up my right hand to clasp theirs in

rapturous hand-shaking, while their voices come ringing down from the gallery, crying, 'Be thou faithful unto death, you shall have a crown.' ''— *Dr. Talmage.*

NATURE OR CHARACTER OF HEAVEN.

Heaven a Place.

"We are accustomed to say that space and time are only conditions of our finite and composite natures, and that to unfettered spirits there would be recognition of neither space nor time. Whether this be true or not, no one can tell. It is a transcendentalism that it is folly to talk about. Time and space are absolute necessities, to our thinking. Every conception of our mind is formed on them as a foundation; and we can have no idea of God Himself, except as in time and space. Hence we must (whether we will or not) take the word 'place' in the passage, 'I go to prepare a place for you,' in a literal sense. Even if it be not literally a place, we think of it as a place, for we cannot think of it in any other way. And, moreover, from the words being used, when our Saviour might have said simply, 'I go to prepare for you,' we may infer that it is actually a place that is meant here. Farther than that perhaps would be

only fancy, and in that region of fancy we cannot
find it profitable to wander. But that on which we
may dwell with profit is, first, that the place is prepared by our Lord; and secondly, that it is prepared for us. What a place must that be which
Christ prepares, which His almighty power and
infinite love combined make ready for our abode!
It must be a place where every purified desire of
the heart must have perpetual satisfaction, and
where Christ's own happiness shall be shared by
those for whom He died. If these are the characteristics of that future home, it makes very little
difference what the spiritual forms of occupation
or the objective elements upheld by the soul in
that better world may be. The inner soul longs
for happiness—it is only the outward and change-
able sense that would dictate its form. That it is
pure and holy, and that it has Christ our Lord and
Saviour in it—this is enough. We know the delicious contents of the vessel, if we do not know
the shape and color of the vessel containing it.
To 'depart' is 'to be with Christ.' "—*Howard
Crosby, D. D., LL.D.*

The Joys of Heaven.

"Death may separate the believer from some

object that he loves, but it draws him nearer to the
object that he mainly loves. It is, indeed, delightful for the believer to think that the friend who first
visited him in his lost estate, and who cherished
him all the way through the wilderness, is the very
friend he is to meet in the Mansion above. Death
does no violence to such a man; It produces no
break in his feelings or affections. Led to love the
Lamb of God when on earth, trained by the Spirit
of God, and by all the dispensations of God, to love
Him more and more, he finds when he has entered
the dark valley and the shadows of death that the
first object that meets his eye, and the most con-
spicuous object, is a Lamb as it has been slain.

" We cannot speak of that which is unspeakable,
or delineate that which is indescribable, and therefore we cannot delineate that joy unspeakable and
full of glory which the believer will enjoy throughout all eternity. The word of God does not furnish
us with any particular account of the holy exer-
cises and joys of heaven. Two very excellent reasons can be given for this: One is, that a vivid
description of the joys of heaven as fascinating the
fancy might rather draw away the mind from the
practical duties of life; and the other is that the
joys of heaven are such that man in his present

state cannot so much as conceive them. Enough
is revealed, however, that the Lamb is slain to be
the grand source of the joys of the saints. There
will be joys springing from the holy affections,
confidence and love, which Christ by His spirit
has planted in the hearts of His people. The
grace, flowing and overflowing and increasing, will
be the source of great and ever-augmented happiness throughout eternity. Again, there will be
joys springing from the glorious society of heaven,
from the company of saints and angels. Brethren
in Christ, you are now walking on the very road
on which all men of God have traveled from creation downwards, and at its termination you shall
meet with all those who have come from the east
and from the west, the north and the south, to sit
down in the kingdom of God. They are one of
many kindred, but they all unite with melody of
voice and heart to sing praises to the Redeemer.
Ye will be in the Heavenly Jerusalem in company
with Jesus, the Mediator of the New Covenant, and
His saints."—*Dr. James McCosh.*

What Heaven Involves.

"The state of eternal glory involves three things:
1. Absence of all sufferring, pain, sin and evil.

2. The presence of all good, both of the purest and
most exalted kind. 3. The complete satisfaction
of all the desires of the soul, at all times through
eternity, without the possibility of decrease on the
one hand, or of satiety on the other, or of any termination of the existence of the receiver or the
received. This is ineffably great and glorious, but
the apostle exceeds all this by saying, 'An heir of
God.' It is therefore not Heaven merely, it is not
the place where no ill can enter, and where pure
and spiritual good is eternally present; it is not
merely a state of endless blessedness in the regions
of glory; it is *God Himself*, God in His plenitude
of glories, God who by the eternal communication
of His glories, meets every wish and satisfies every
desire of a deathless and imperishable spirit, which
He has created for Himself, and of which Himself
is the only portion. To a soul composed of infinite
desires, what would the place or state called
'Heaven' be, if God were not there? God, then
is the portion of the soul, and the only portion
with which its infinite powers can be satisfied.
How wonderful is his lot! A child of corruption,
lately a slave of sin and heir of perdition, tossed
about with every storm of life; in afflictions many
and privations oft; having perhaps scarcely where

to lay his head; and at last prostrated by death
and mingled with the dust of the earth: but now,
how changed! The soul is renewed in glory, the
body fashioned after the glorious human nature of
Jesus Christ, and both joined together in an in-
destructible bond, clearer than the moon, brighter
than the sun, and more resplendent than all the
heavenly spheres, and having overcome through
the grace of Christ, is set down with Jesus on his
throne to reign forever and ever."—*Dr. Adam
Clarke.*

The Vision of Deity.

"In many inspired descriptions of heaven, the
Shekinah, or the visible presence of God, is made
prominent. This might be expected if the anti-
type corresponds with the type; and if Heaven be
an advance stage of the manifestations of the Deity
to man, we should look for a richer display of the
divine glory and a more perfect consciousness of
the divine presence. Hence the city selected to
prefigure the eternal residence was not the classic
Athens nor imperial Rome, though adorned with
statuary, studded with temples, rich in historic
fame. No, but the capital of Judea, because there
Jehovah's presence was wont to be displayed to
His worshippers. Yet this is the New Jerusalem,

because of its purity and the richer glory which fills
it as the shrine of the divine Majesty. 'And I saw
no temple therein,' says the enraptured John, as
he gazes on its unearthly radiance; 'I saw no
temple therein, for the Lord God Almighty and the
Lamb are the temple of it. And the city had no
need of the sun, neither of the moon to shine in it;
for the glory of God did lighten it, and the Lamb
is the light thereof.' The allusion here cannot be
misunderstood. In the Holy of Holies of the
earthly Jerusalem there was neither natural nor
artificial light; no golden lamp shone within its
walls, and not a ray of the sun could enter there,
for that sacred place was illumined by the glory of
the Shekinah, which occasionally filled the temple
with supernatural brightness, and shone forth to
the view of the joyful crowd of worshippers without. So in the heavenly city the sun and moon
shed not their rays, nor is there need for the reflection or emission of light from any natural
luminary, because the actual personal presence of
Jehovah fills it with glory. Even the temple itself
is dispensed with in the Celestial City, because the
vision of God is there unveiled, and access to Him
is without the intervention of symbolic rites. The
earthly temple, while forming a shrine for the

20

Shekinah, was a mode of concealment from the view of the people. The glory was curtained off and shut in, so that the radiant symbol was en-throned in solitary majesty in the most holy place. But in the New Jerusalem no temple is seen, for no external shade is required ; and in the brightness of a better dispensation concealment and restriction have disappeared. In leaving earth the spirits of the just leave the outer court and enter within the veil, into the Holy of Holies—into Heaven itself, the presence of the divine Majesty—and live con-tinually within its brightness. No walls there form a barrier between God and His people, not even the temple walls, not even the veil of the temple, for the saints dwell in His immediate pres-ence. No cloud shrouds His radiant majesty from their gaze, but they all with open face behold His glory, and there is neither darkness nor distance between them and God.

"Nor are the representations of the saints, as dwelling in the divine presence, to be denuded of their import by the cold criticism that would re-solve them into mere figures of speech. The type and symbol belong to earth, the divine reality be-longs to heaven. In speaking of believers dwelling in the divine presence, the Scriptures mean an actual dwelling and an actual presence. In speaking of the saints seeing God, they mean an actual view of the Deity. The benediction promise of the Saviour is, 'Blessed are the pure in heart, for they shall see God;' the prayer of the Saviour is, 'That they may behold my glory which thou hast given me;' and the promise that immediately follows the description of the blessed in the New Jerusalem is, 'And they shall see His face.' These refer to a true and proper vision of the Deity. As certainly as the Jews of old saw the symbol of God's presence when it filled the sanctuary; as certainly as Moses saw the glory of God from the cleft of the rock; as certainly as Moses and Elias saw the Redeemer on the Mount of Transfiguration; as really as the high priest entered the Holy of Holies, and saw the radiant cloud between the cherubim over the mercy seat, so truly shall the saints enter Heaven and see the Deity face to face. They shall dwell where He is; they shall see Him as He is. For then, 'behold the tabernacle of God is with men, and He will dwell with them, and they shall be His people, and God Himself shall be with them, and be their God.'

"Here, then, is the first consummation of the believer's hopes and aspirations. At last the wilderness is left, and the promised paradise is gained; the weary pilgrim has arrived at home; the absent son and heir has entered his father's house. The journey of faith ends in realizing vision and actual possession. On earth he loved the Saviour with supreme affection, though he saw him not—'whom having not seen yet he loved; in whom, though he saw him not, yet believing he rejoiced with joy unspeakable and full of glory.' Satisfied with God as his portion, he exclaims, 'Whom have I in Heaven but Thee? and there is none in earth that I desire beside Thee.' But love longs for the sight and presence of its object, and while faith and hope anticipate, love stimulates the desire for the happy hour of realization and possession, and the bitterest sorrows and the deepest sufferings are patiently endured under its expectation. Now is that hour come. The happy spirit is with Christ, sees Him, at sight of Him eternity opens with ever-during bliss. O what a recompense for all our sorrows, conflicts and tears, will be found in the first moment we have of gazing on the glorified Saviour! Well, poor, tempted, tried, despised and persecuted believer, be patient a little longer, persevere through a few more conflicts and sorrows, and thy Lord shall call thee home, and thou shalt be forever with Him to behold the King in His beauty, and the land that is afar off."—*Wm. Cooke, D. D.*

"O holy dwelling-place of God!
  O glorious city all divine !
Thy streets, by feet of seraphs trod,
  Shall one glad day be trod by mine.

"In Thee no temple lifts its dome,
  No sun its radiant beam lets fall ;
For there, of light the eternal home,
  God and the Lamb illumine all!

"There from exhaustless fountains flow
  The living waters, gushing o'er,
Which whoso drinks thenceforth shall know
  Earth's ever-craving thirst no more.

"There fresh and fair on every hand,
  Where one unfading summer lives,
The trees of life unwithering stand,
  Whose fruit immortal vigor gives.

"All lovelier flowers than Eden bare
  When God pronounced His work complete,
All matchless forms of beauty, there
  The never-wearied eye shall greet.

"Within the burnished gates abide
  Of God's redeemed the countless throng,
Who ever while the ages glide
  Serve in seraphic ardor strong.

"To them the Lamb that fills the throne
　In love divine unveils His face;
　While they, with bliss to earth unknown,
　Adore the beauty and the grace.

"No wasting sorrow there is found,
　No cheek is wet with burning tears;
　Whom those eternal walls surround,
　No foe can reach, no pang, no fears.

"Land of the blest, on faith's keen eye
　Faint glimpses of thy glory break;
　Oh, when in earth's last sleep I lie,
　Mid thy full splendors let me wake!"

—Ray Palmer, D. D.

www.ingramcontent.com/pod-product-compliance
Lightning Source LLC
Chambersburg PA
CBHW031407270326
41929CB00010BA/1357